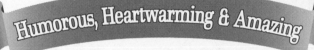

Humorous, Heartwarming & Amazing

DOG TRIVIA

Wendy Pirk

BLUE
BIKE
BOOKS

The Publisher: Blue Bike Books

Website: www.bluebikebooks.com

Library and Archives Canada Cataloguing in Publication

Pirk, Wendy, 1973–
        Dog trivia : humorous, heartwarming & amazing / written by
Wendy Pirk; illustrated by Peter Tyler.

ISBN-13: 978-1-897278-36-9
ISBN-10: 1-897278-36-5

        1. Dogs—Miscellanea. I. Tyler, Peter, 1976– III. Title.
SF426.2.P57 2008   636.7   C2007-905987-2

Project Director: Nicholle Carrière
Project Editor: Pat Price
Photos Courtesy of: Photos.com; p.6 (Wendy Pirk)
Illustrations: Peter Tyler

PC: P5

We acknowledge the support of the Alberta Foundation for the Arts for
our publishing program.

DEDICATION

To my family, because without them, I am nothing.
And to those who work tirelessly to improve the situation for dogs
and other animals worldwide: Keep up the good work.

ACKNOWLEDGEMENTS

Thanks first and foremost to my editor, Pat Price, for her patience, hard work and sharp eye, and to Nicholle Carrière for giving me the opportunity to write this book (and for not kicking me to the curb, though I'm sure she was sorely tempted to do so on more than one occasion).

Thanks also to my long-suffering friends, who probably reached a point where they would have preferred to duck into the shrubbery when they saw me coming, rather than listen to me rattle off yet another batch of dog factoids. No more canine minutia, I promise.

And thanks to Smiley, who makes my life better just by being in it.

CONTENTS

INTRODUCTION 7

MEET THE FAMILY
Ancestral Canines. 8
All in the Family. 11
Canine Cousins 18
You Call that a Dog? 23
Man's Best Friend. 25

CANINE DESIGN
Inside and Out 28
A Cure for What Ails You 35
Record-breaking Pups. 41

DOGS OF DISTINCTION
A Breed or Not a Breed?. 45
Sheepdogs and Cattle Dogs (except Swiss Cattle Dogs) 46
Pinschers, Schnauzers, Molossians,
Swiss Mountain Dogs and Swiss Cattle Dogs. 49
Terriers 52
Dachshunds 53
Spitzes and Primitive Dogs. 54
Scent Hounds and Related Breeds 57
Pointing Dogs. 59
Retrievers, Flushing Dogs and Water Dogs 61
Companion and Toy Dogs. 63
Sighthounds 66
Provisionally Accepted Breeds. 68
Unrecognized Breeds 69

THE CANINE HALL OF FAME
Real Dogs. 70
Behind Every Great Person is a Great Dog. 77
VIPs (Very Important Pooches) 82
Dogs with Star Power. 86

DOGS IN POPULAR CULTURE
Pups in Print. 89
Canine Classics. 92
Contemporary Canine Tales. 94
Dogs on Stage and Screen. 96

Dogs on the Tube 98
Reel Dogs 102

DOGS IN THE NEWS
Miscellaneous Mutt Stories 106
Heroic Hounds 109
Dogs Behaving Badly 112
Amazing Feats 116
What Were They Thinking? 118

CANINE FOLKLORE
Who's Afraid of the Big, Bad Werewolf? 123
More Paranormal Pooches 127
Doggone Superstitions 130
Mythological Mutts 132

MORAL TAILS: CANINE FABLES
Aesop's Fables 140
Krasicki's Fables 147

DOGISMS
Dog Words 148
Doggie Expressions 151

PROFESSIONAL PUPS
The Dogs of War 157
Rescue Dogs 160
Sniffer Dogs 162
Police Dogs 164
Draft Animals 166
Assistance Dogs 169

PAMPERED POOCHES
Canine Couture 174
Pampered Pooch Products 178
Doggie Services 182

A GLOBAL PERSPECTIVE
Ruff Treatment 186
Dog Laws 192
Strange Dog Laws 196
Dog Names 198
Mutt Miscellanea 201

ABOUT THE ILLUSTRATOR 207
ABOUT THE AUTHOR 208

"The one absolutely unselfish friend that man can have in this selfish world, the one that never deserts him, the one that never proves ungrateful or treacherous, is his DOG. A man's dog stands by him in prosperity and in poverty, in health and in sickness. He will sleep on the cold ground, where the wintry winds blow and the snow drives fiercely, if only he may be near his master's side. He will kiss the hand that has no food to offer, he will lick the wounds and sores that come in encounters with the roughness of the world. He guards the sleep of his pauper master as if he were a prince. When all other friends desert, he remains. When riches take wing and reputation falls to pieces, he is as constant in his love as the sun in its journey through the heavens...."

–George Vest, 1870

INTRODUCTION

There's a reason we refer to dogs as "man's best friend" (or, to be politically correct, "humanity's best friend"). No other animal has had such a long or close association with people. Dogs were around long before people settled into permanent communities and cultivated crops. They hunted alongside us, defended our settlements, warned us of impending danger and kept us company.

Today, our canine cohorts dig us out of avalanches, track us in the wilderness when we get lost, protect us from harm—and even serve as our arms and legs when ours are incapable of functioning. Best of all, though, they are our companions, our good friends, who never consider it beneath their dignity to come running, tails wagging, bodies vibrating with excitement, to give us sloppy, dog-breath kisses the moment we walk through the door.

In return, we feed them, walk them, hug them and play endless rounds of tug-of-war. We also, as you'll find out in the following pages, dress them up in bunny slippers, send them to doggie massage therapists and shower them with all-natural treats from the doggie bakery.

This book won't tell you how to potty train your pup or know a Shar Pei from a Shih Tzu. But it will tell you what a dogsbody is and what national leader used a crystal ball to communicate with his dear departed pooch, plus a whole lot more weird and wonderful doggie trivia.

So curl up with your best friend and read on. Because, as Charles Schulz once said, "Happiness is a warm puppy."

ANCESTRAL CANINES

Domestic dogs as we know them today are more the result of human tinkering with genetics than evolution. At no time in the past would you have seen a pack of wild Chihuahuas or toy poodles prowling the landscape, stalking and bringing down an animal for food. Nope, these little pups exist today solely because people wanted little companion pooches to lavish with affection. In fact, most of our domestic dog breeds exist because, at some point in the past, someone had a specific role in mind that they wanted a canine to fill, so dogs were selectively bred until a pup came along with just the right traits. If people hadn't meddled with their genetics, domestic dogs would probably still look like their wild ancestor, the wolf. And where did wolves come from? Well, I'm glad you asked...

Lions and Tigers and Bears, Oh My!

According to palaeontologists, canines, bears, raccoons, civets, hyenas and felines all share a common ancestor—*Miacis,* a genus of weasel-like animals that lived on the European and North American continents approximately 65 to 42 million years ago, during the late Paleocene and early Eocene epochs.

Miacids had retractable claws, hind limbs that were longer than their forelimbs and binocular vision. They were most likely arboreal, living in forested habitats and preying on small mammals and birds.

The Big Split

Roughly 40 million years ago, the *Miacis* genus split into two branches—one of bear-like mammals and one of dog-like animals called *Cynodictis.* Characteristics that these prehistoric canines shared with their modern-day descendants include the presence of anal glands and the same number of teeth. Although *Cynodictis* species still had five toes, the fifth toe was already beginning to shorten into what would eventually become the dewclaw in species farther down the evolutionary line. Native to North America, *Cynodictis* spent most of its time in grassy plains, though it might have hunted for prey in trees. It likely looked a lot like the modern-day civet.

Top Dogs

If you were punted back in time 10 to 12 million years and, while strolling across the grasslands of North America, ran into a member of the *Epicyon* genus, you would be in big trouble. These huge canids were some of the top predators of their time. Classified as "bone-crushing dogs," *Epicyon* had many traits in common with the modern-day hyena. *Epicyon haydeni*, which was the size of a large black bear, was the largest canid to have ever lived.

Hey, Buddy, How's it Going?

Another canine ancestor worthy of note is the species *Tomarctus,* which lived about 10 million years ago in the grasslands of North America and is believed to be the first social canid. Wolves, coyotes, jackals and domestic dogs are direct descendants of *Tomarctus.*

Dire Straits

The dire wolf (*Canis dirus*) is an extinct canid that lived during the Pleistocene epoch. It looked much like the gray wolf, except that it was larger and had shorter limbs. The dire wolf was about 5 feet (1.5 meters) long and is thought to have weighed between 120 and 175 pounds (55 and 80 kilograms). It coexisted with the gray wolf in North America for almost 100,000 years and died out about 10,000 years ago.

Although the dire wolf was bigger than other North American wolves, paleozoologists believe that it was not as swift as other wolf species. When the large, slower-moving Pleistocene mega-fauna started dying out about 16,000 years ago, the dire wolf lost its main sources of prey and most likely became a scavenger.

DID YOU KNOW?

Most of the dire wolf fossils that have been recovered were found in the La Brea Tar Pits in California.

What's Hiding in Them Thar Hills?

Although the dire wolf is thought to have become extinct about 10,000 years ago, fossils found in the Ozarks, Arkansas, suggest that a relic population may have existed in the region as recently as 4000 years ago.

ALL IN THE FAMILY

There are between 35 and 38 species in the Canidae family (those wacky taxonomists can't agree on anything), excluding those that have become extinct. All canids share common characteristics — they have similar dental structures, walk on their toes rather than the soles of their feet and have long tails and snouts. Some people, however, get a little carried away with categorizing the species, distinguishing "wolf-like dogs," which they attribute to the genus Canis, *from other dogs.*

Gray Wolf (*Canis lupus*)

The direct ancestor of all domestic dogs, the gray wolf was once common throughout North America, Europe and Asia but is now listed as threatened or endangered in much of its range. Also known as the timber wolf, the gray wolf is the largest member of the dog family, sporting bigger paws, longer legs, a longer muzzle and larger teeth than its canine cousins. The gray wolf is a social animal and lives in packs that vary in size from 2 to 20 animals. Each pack has a social hierarchy that is dominated by the alpha male and female.

DID YOU  KNOW?

Wolves have scent glands between their toes, so they can mark their territory as they patrol it.

And the Howls Have it!

When people think of wolves, what first comes to mind is their beautiful, eerie howling. Each wolf has a distinct howl that allows other members of its pack to identify it, and an adult wolf will respond only to the call of a wolf that it knows (except the alpha pair, which may challenge an unknown wolf calling in their territory). Wolf pups will respond indiscriminately to calls they hear, probably because they have not yet learned to identify the calls of the other wolves in their pack.

Wolves howl not only to communicate with other members of their own pack but also to let other packs know that they are in the area. Rival packs use howling choruses to gauge each other's location and pack size. Based on the information they learn from each other's chorus, the packs may choose to avoid confrontation and slide quietly around each other, or one pack may decide to challenge the other if it believes the rival pack is smaller.

A wolf separated from its pack has a difficult decision to make: should it howl, so it can reunite with its pack or stay quiet to avoid rival packs? Rival pack members might follow the howl back to its source and kill the lone wolf. One of the most common causes of death for adult wolves is being killed by members of a rival pack.

DID YOU  **KNOW?**

A wolf's howl can carry as far as 10 miles (6 kilometers).

Coyote (*Canis latrans*)

The coyote, also known as the prairie wolf, is found only in North America, its range stretching from the Arctic to Panama. Originally a western species, it has slowly been working its way eastward across the continent. The coyote looks very much like a wolf but with a thinner, more pointed muzzle, larger ears and feet that are small in proportion to the rest of its body.

Like wolves, coyotes communicate by howling (if you can call the yippy sounds they make howling). Once a chorus is started, coyotes will readily respond to recorded howls and even to human imitations, though once they figure out that they're not communicating with another coyote, they tend to stop howling altogether and wait for the impostor to fall quiet before they continue. Coyotes also stop calling if they hear a wolf howl. In urban areas, coyotes can often be heard "serenading" the sirens of emergency vehicles, such as police cruisers and ambulances.

An exceptionally adaptable species, the coyote has actually benefited from the presence of humans and is common in rural (and increasingly in urban) areas. Most of its diet is made up of small mammals, especially rodents, but it will eat almost anything, including insects, eggs and small birds. Where it coexists with humans, the coyote has expanded its culinary palate to include domestic fowl, food scraps, the contents of garbage cans and compost heaps, and pet cats and dogs. Coyotes have even been seen digging in backyard gardens and snacking on the vegetables. So, maybe you shouldn't be so quick to blame the bunnies the next time your carrot patch is raided…

DID YOU KNOW?

Coyotes that live in arid areas in which the coyote melon (*Cucurbita foetidissima*) grows make it a regular part of their diet. They are one of only two animals that will eat this fruit (the other is the peccary). Perhaps other species are put off by the coyote melon's distinct "underarm" smell. I can't image why…

Golden Jackal (*Canis aureus*)

Largest of the jackal species, the golden jackal is named for its golden-tipped fur. Resembling a coyote, the jackal could almost be considered the North American canid's Old World equivalent, because it fills a similar ecological niche, scavenging and hunting small rodents in its native Africa. Also found in the Balkan Peninsula, Thailand and Sri Lanka, the golden jackal is the only jackal species that occurs outside of northern and eastern Africa.

Golden jackals do not form packs. Pairs mate for life and work together to defend their territory. Pups from previous litters often stay with the parents to help raise and protect the next litter. A favorite food item of hyenas, leopards and even eagles, most golden jackal pups don't make it past the first two or three months.

DID YOU  **KNOW?**

The jackal is mentioned many times in the Bible, always in a negative context, as in "be a good Christian or you will turn into a jackal." Clearly the ancients were not big jackal fans.

 Evolutionarily speaking, a canine's bark is an alarm call that is meant to signal other members of its pack. Domestic dogs' barks are sharper and louder than their wild cousins', and they tend to bark more often.

Golden Jackal Cross

In 1975, a Russian researcher named Klim Sulimov began breeding golden jackals with Siberian huskies. His goal was to create an animal with the jackal's sense of smell and the husky's friendly disposition and tolerance to cold temperatures, making it an ideal sniffer dog for the cold Russian climate. His breeding program was successful, and the resulting species is known as the Sulimov dog.

Dingo
(Canis lupus dingo)
The dingo, also known as the warrigal, is a medium-sized dog with a reddish coat, pointy ears and a blunt muzzle. It is believed to be a direct descendant of the Indian wolf and can be found in southeast Asia, as well as in central and western Australia. Although it is generally thought to be an Australian dog, the dingo isn't a native species and was introduced to the continent sometime between 3000 and 4000 years ago. As is the case with many introduced species, the arrival of the dingo is believed to have had a disastrous effect on some of Australia's native species—it might have driven the country's marsupial carnivores to extinction. Listed as a vulnerable species, the dingo itself is now at risk, because it is interbreeding with domestic dogs.

DID YOU KNOW?

Australian dingoes are much larger than their Asian counterparts, probably because Asian dingoes survive mostly on garbage, instead of hunting for themselves.

DOG FACT
On average, a wolf will break 29 percent of its teeth over the course of its life by biting or chewing on bones.

Ethiopian Wolf (*Canis simensis*)

The Ethiopian wolf, once known as the Simien jackal, is one of the most endangered animals on the planet, with fewer than 500 left in the wild. This species is restricted to a few mountain ranges in Ethiopia, and it is the only wolf in sub-Saharan Africa. Although it looks more like a long-legged red fox than a wolf, the Ethiopian wolf likely descended from the gray wolves that crossed into Africa during the last Ice Age and were stranded when the ice disappeared.

The Ethiopian wolf is a social animal, but its social structure differs from that of other canines, in which there are more females than males, because the less-dominant males leave their birth pack to establish packs of their own. Ethiopian wolf packs include twice as many males as females, and males tend to stay in the pack into which they were born, while the females sometimes branch out into other packs. The alpha female is the only one that breeds, but she is not monogamous and might mate with males from other packs, as well as the alpha male from her own pack.

DID YOU KNOW?

Unlike the alpha male, the alpha female in an Ethiopian wolf pack does not have to compete for her position; she remains alpha until she dies, at which time the beta female moves up to take her place.

> *A dog is the only thing on earth that loves you*
> *more than he loves himself.*
>
> –Josh Billings

CANINE COUSINS

*Although they may not be "wolf-like," many canine
species are "dog-like" and are easily recognizable as
cousins of our furry domesticated friends.*

Red Fox
(*Vulpes vulpes*)

Sly, cunning and clever are some of the words often used to describe the red fox. Perhaps resourceful is another word that should be added to the list. This fox is the most wide-spread carnivore in the world and can be found throughout most of North America, Europe and Asia, as well as in Australia and northern Africa, where it is still expanding its range. The red fox has a red to reddish brown coat, white belly, long, bushy, white-tipped tail and pointy, black-tipped ears. It eats mostly rodents, rabbits and insects but is an opportunist and will take almost any prey it can catch.

DID YOU  KNOW?

To stay warm in cold weather, the red fox will curl up and cover itself with its long, bushy tail.

Maned Wolf (*Chrysocyon brachyurus*)

Despite its name, the maned wolf looks less like a wolf than a shaggy, overgrown red fox with long, spindly legs and a bad haircut. Its mane is a thatch of black hair that stretches across the dog's shoulders, making it look even scruffier. Even though it is the largest canine in South America, with its big ears, delicate-looking legs and overall unkempt appearance, this wolf does not exactly instill fear in the hearts of those who see it.

Like the fox and the coyote, the maned wolf is opportunistic when it comes to food. It hunts small mammals, especially rodents, birds, reptiles and insects, and it also eats fish, fruit and vegetation. It is especially fond of bananas and a tomato-like fruit called the *lobeira*. When hunting rodents, the maned wolf taps the ground with its front paw to flush out its prey, then captures it with a fox-like pounce.

DID YOU KNOW?

When the maned wolf feels threatened, it puffs up its mane to make itself look bigger, sort of like the canine equivalent of a blowfish.

African Wild Dog (*Lycaon pictus*)

Also known as the painted wolf, the Cape hunting dog, and the African hunting dog, the African wild dog is found only in Africa, in the savannas south of the Sahara desert. With its rounded ears, black face and mottled coat, it is easily confused with the hyena. The pattern of an African wild dog's coat is unique to the individual, much like a zebra and its stripes. This dog is the second-most endangered carnivore in Africa, after the Ethiopian wolf.

The African wild dog hunts in packs, usually chasing down ungulates such as impala and gazelles, but it will not turn up its nose at other prey species, if it can catch them. This species puts the lion to shame with its success rate in hunting; the wild dog catches its prey 70 to 90 percent of the time, whereas the "King of the Beasts" catches only a paltry 30 percent.

Thought to be the most social of canine species, the African wild dog has some unique pack behaviors. Pups that join in the hunt actually get to eat before the adults, and pack members will return to the den site and regurgitate meat for animals that are too old or infirm to join in the hunt. The wild dog communicates with its pack members with a squeaky, bird-like chirp.

DID YOU KNOW?

African wild dogs have only four toes on their front feet. They do not have the dewclaw that all other dog species have.

Bat-eared Fox *(Otocyon megalotis)*

The bat-eared fox has been around since the Pleistocene epoch, when it could be found in parts of Asia and Africa. Today, this canine is limited to the savannas and grasslands of south and east Africa. Easily recognizable by its enormous ears and black, raccoon-like face mask, the bat-eared fox eats mostly insects, especially termites, and can often be found lurking near herds of zebra or antelope to snack on the insects that land in their dung. It will also catch the odd rodent or bird and sometimes eats fruit. This fox is nocturnal and relies on its hearing, rather than its vision, to find prey.

 Dogs and wolves yawn when they are content, not because they are sleepy.

DID YOU KNOW?

The bat-eared fox has the most teeth of all the dog species (as many as 50).

Fennec (*Vulpes zerda*)

Another big-eared fox of Africa and Asia is the fennec. The smallest member of the canine family—it's smaller than the average housecat—it has the biggest ears, beating out even the bat-eared fox, which says a lot. The fennec is native to the Sahara Desert and has fur on the soles of its feet to protect them from the scorching desert sand. Because it gets most of the moisture it needs from its food, it can go a long time without drinking. Fennecs are social animals, living in packs called "harems." It is the only species of fox that has been domesticated and is sometimes kept as a pet.

DID YOU KNOW?

Fennecs can jump distances of up to four times their own body length.

If you pick up a starving dog and make him prosperous, he will not bite you. This is the principal difference between a dog and a man.

–Mark Twain

YOU CALL THAT A DOG?

Some members of the Canidae *family look so little
like dogs that you would never suspect they are
genetically related.*

The Raccoon Dog (*Nyctereutes procyonoides*)

If it looks like a raccoon, and acts like a raccoon, it must be a…
dog? It is not hard to see how the raccoon dog got its name—in
appearance, it's more raccoon than dog. In fact, I don't even
need to provide a description for this animal: just picture a large
raccoon, give it a slightly more canine shape, and voila, you have
the raccoon dog.

This species is also known as the *tanuki* throughout much of its
range. It is native to Japan and Manchuria but was introduced
to the European continent in the mid-1900s for hunting and
can now be found throughout Scandinavia, Germany and
France. Like the raccoon, the raccoon dog is omnivorous and
adaptable, dining on whatever is readily available in its habitat.

DID YOU KNOW?

The raccoon dog is the only canine that goes into a hibernation-
like state to conserve energy in cold weather. Its defense strategy
is also unusual for a dog—it plays dead when it feels threatened.

The Bush Dog (*Speothos venaticus*)

The bush dog's appearance has been described as similar to an
otter, a weasel or a badger, but, personally, I think it looks more
like a bear cub, especially in the face. It has reddish brown fur,
a stocky body with stumpy little legs, webbed feet, small ears
and a short, bushy tail. Its muzzle is shorter than you would

expect for a dog, which may explain why the bush dog has the fewest teeth of all canine species (38, instead of the usual 42).

Bush dogs live in the wet savannas and tropical forests of Panama, Columbia, Venezuela, Brazil, Argentina, Bolivia, Peru and Guyana. Although they have a wide distribution, they are rare and are listed as vulnerable to extinction. Bush dogs prey mostly on rodents, especially pacas and agoutis. Strong swimmers, they will chase and take down their prey in streams and rivers.

One strong wolf cannot defeat a pack of dogs; one strong arm cannot defeat many fists.

–Chinese proverb

MAN'S BEST FRIEND

All domestic dogs share a common ancestor, the gray wolf. Differences in the DNA of domestic dogs and wolves have led scientists to believe that the domestic dog split from its wolf ancestor roughly 100,000 years ago.

DID YOU KNOW?

Wolves and coyotes share 94 percent of their mitochondrial DNA, while wolves and dogs share 99 percent.

In the Beginning

No one really knows when or how dogs were domesticated. Some suggest that early pastoralists tamed the wolf intentionally, to use it as a working dog, while another school of thought has it that domestication was more serendipitous—wolves approached human settlements to feed on waste piles, and people realized the advantages of having the big dogs around.

The remains of domestic dogs that date back 14,000 years have been discovered in Iraq; bones dating back 12,000 years were uncovered in France; and remains found in China are at least 10,000 years old. Wolf bones that are 100,000 years old have been found with human bones dating to the same time, but the relationship between wolf and human has not been determined.

A Boy and His Dog

France's Chauvet Cave is famous for its Paleolithic paintings. In 2004, researchers discovered tracks in Chauvet Cave that they believe belong to a prehistoric dog. Until this finding, the oldest known tracks were from a site in Germany and dated back 12,000 years. The tracks at Chauvet Cave are closer to 26,000 years old and—drum roll, please—they are associated with human footprints. Researchers believe the human tracks are those of a young boy, perhaps 10 years old. From the way the two sets of tracks are intertwined, researchers believe the boy and the dog were walking together when they visited the cave, but this has not yet been proven.

What's in a Name?

The archaeological record proves that ancient Egyptians kept dogs as pets. Egyptologists have uncovered leather collars with nametags and discovered dog names carved into stone stelae (decorative pillars or slabs) and reliefs. Some dogs were named for their physical characteristics—Blacky, for example—some were simply given numbers, and others were named for the dogs' personality traits or capabilities: Brave One, Reliable, Good Herdsman, Antelope and even Useless are just a few.

Just a Little Off the Top, Please

According to the Greek historian Herodotus, ancient Egyptians thought so highly of their dogs that when the pet passed away, the family members shaved their heads and entire bodies in mourning. The dog would then be buried in a sacred place.

DID YOU  KNOW?

Ancient Egyptians swore "by the dog" when making promises they wouldn't break.

All that Remains

Thanks again to that trusty old archaeological record, we know that ancient Romans also kept pet dogs. Mosaics have been uncovered in the city of Pompeii that read "*cave canem*," the Latin equivalent of "beware of dog."

Further evidence from the ruined city comes in the form of the famous dog "cavity." When Mount Vesuvius erupted in 79 AD, a thick layer of ash buried the city and everyone in it. The bodies eventually decomposed, leaving behind cavities in the hardened blanket of ash. Archaeologists made casts from these cavities, and one such cast was of a pet watchdog. The unlucky pooch was wearing a bronze-studded collar and was chained up outside his master's house.

The dog wags his tail, not for you, but for your bread.

–Portuguese proverb

INSIDE AND OUT

*The original canine form (before humans started breed-
ing dogs for specific traits) was designed for strength and
speed. The same can hardly be said today, at least, for
many domestic dog breeds. I may be underestimating our
furry friends, but I suspect the day will never come when
a Basset hound takes home the "speedy dog of the year"
award, or a Chinese crested wows the crowd with a stun-
ning feat of strength. And that's okay, because a dog is so
much more than just the sum of its parts.*

Baritone or Soprano?

It is not the size of a dog's body that determines the "yippiness"
of its bark; it is the length of the dog's neck. Neck length determines the size of the dog's vocal cords, which in turn influences
the pitch and loudness of a dog's voice when it barks and howls.
The shorter the neck, the yippier the dog's bark.

The Leg Bone's Connected to the…

Dogs, on average, have 321 bones in their body. This number varies from breed to breed, depending on the length of the dog's tail. A short tail can have as few as six vertebrae, whereas a long tail can have as many as 23.

DID YOU KNOW?

A dog's body has 13 sets of ribs, and seven bones, called cervical vertebrae, support its neck.

How *You* Doin'?

A dog uses his tail for more than just balance—he also uses it to express himself. A happy, confident dog holds his tail high and wags it with a slow, sweeping motion. A dog that is scared or anxious holds his tail down, sometimes tucking it between his legs, and might wag the tip with a quick, agitated motion.

Collarless

Unlike humans, dogs do not have collarbones. Their shoulder bones "float," allowing dogs to take longer strides when they run and leap.

Canine Choppers

Adult dogs have 42 teeth—six pairs of incisors, two pairs of canines or fangs, eight pairs of premolars and five pairs of molars. Puppies have only 28 teeth. Because they don't yet need to grind their food, they do not have the molars. Puppies generally get their permanent teeth at three to four months of age.

In the 16th century, dog saliva was thought to have healing properties.

What Soft Fur You Have

Most dog breeds have two types of coat hair: a thick, warm undercoat hair and a coarse outer coat, or guard hair, which acts as a sort of weatherproofing. How soft and snuggly little Fido is depends on his coat's ratio of undercoat hair to guard hair; if the undercoat hair is denser or longer than the guard hair, Fido will be soft like a teddy bear, but if the guard hair is more prominent, you might as well be hugging a Brillo pad. Well, maybe it's not quite that bad, but he certainly won't be taking home any "Softest Fur of the Year" awards.

DID YOU KNOW?

Adult dogs use their incisors for grooming each other, as well as gnawing and nibbling on bones.

Hoover-free Hound

Some breeds, such as greyhounds and poodles, are single-coated, having only the coarser guard hairs. Because they have no thick undercoat, these dogs shed much less than their double-coated relatives, making them good pets for people who suffer from allergies (and for those of us who hate to vacuum).

Who Are You Calling Hairless?

Dogs with dense coats, such as Alaskan malamutes or Samoyeds, can have as many as 610 hairs per inch (240 per centimeter). Fine-haired pooches, such as Afghans, may have fewer than 254 per inch (100 per centimeter). Most of the "hairless" breeds are not in fact hairless; they usually have wispy patches of hair somewhere on their body, usually the head. The only breed that truly lives up to the "hairless" label is the American hairless terrier, a follically challenged version of the rat terrier.

The Better to Sense You With

A dog's whiskers are just hairs that are longer and more than twice as thick as the hair that covers the rest of its body. Although the whiskers themselves have no nerves (they are just hairs, after all), they are attached to a huge bundle of sensory receptors. Whiskers help a dog interact with its environment by picking up vibrations in air currents.

DID YOU  KNOW?

Whiskers are among the first hairs to grow in puppies.

The Nose Knows

With only about 1700 taste buds in their tongues (compared to 9000, which is how many humans have), you might expect dogs to have a poor sense of taste. Not true. Taste and sense of smell are closely related, and a canine nose has more than 200 million scent receptors (compared to our 5 million). This allows wild dogs to distinguish between safe and unsafe foods in their environment, and it allows your pup to distinguish between his yummy canned dog food and the nasty heartworm pill you tried to hide in it.

No Need to Shout

A dog's ear has about 30 muscles, which allow him to move his ears to track a sound. Canines hear far better than humans. Dogs can hear sounds with frequencies of up to 45 kHz, whereas our relatively feeble hearing only registers sounds of up to 23 kHz. As well as hearing higher-pitched sounds, dogs can hear sounds that are far away, as much as four times farther than those we can hear.

The Better to Smell You With

Ever wonder why Fido's nose is damp? It is not a sign of good health, as popular wisdom would have you believe. The moisture on a dog's nose captures and dissolves airborne molecules, helping to trap scents.

DID YOU KNOW?

One-third of a dog's brain is used to detect scents.

Why Stop at Two?

As well as an upper and lower eyelid, dogs have a third eyelid that is tucked between the other two and sweeps across the eye from the inner corner. It helps to keep the surface of the eye clean, sort of like an optical windshield wiper.

The Eyes Have It

While their range is not as great as humans', dogs can see in color, not just in black and white, as is generally believed. If we had the same color vision as dogs, it would seem to us that we were living in perpetual dusk, which for dogs is okay, because they see best in dim light, and their night vision kicks butt. The canine eye is also far better at detecting movement, especially with its peripheral vision, but it does not focus as well as the human eye on stationary objects.

DID YOU  KNOW?

Puppies of all breeds are born with blue eyes, which change into the breed's standard color as the puppies mature.

Be Still, My Beating Heart

While all dogs' hearts race in anticipation from time to time, they race at different speeds, depending on the dog's breed. Small dogs have a pulse of 140 to 160 beats per minute; a medium dog's pulse, at 120 to 140 beats per minute, is somewhat slower; and a large breed's pulse is slower still, at only 60 to 80 beats per minute. Puppies of all breeds have a pulse of up to 180 beats per minute until they are a year old.

Under the Armpit, Please!

A healthy body temperature for a dog ranges from 100.5 to 102.5°F (38 to 39.2°C). The best way to determine canine body temperature is with a rectal thermometer (sorry, pooch!); feeling your dog's nose to see if it is warm or dry doesn't actually tell you anything. A body temperature of 108°F (42°C) or higher can be fatal. The heart, brain, kidney, liver and intestines begin to break down, and the damage is largely irreversible.

No Doggie Deodorant for Me

Dogs pant to bring their body temperature down. Instead of sweating from the skin's surface, as humans do, moisture evaporates from the surface of the tongue and from the bottoms of their paws.

DID YOU  KNOW?

A healthy dog at rest takes 18 to 34 breaths per minute.

Puppies Aplenty

Most dog breeds can have two litters of puppies a year. The female's pregnancy lasts about two months, and a typical litter size ranges from 6 to 10 puppies. The age at which a female starts having estrus cycles varies by breed; smaller dogs generally begin by the time they are six months old, whereas larger breeds may not begin until they are almost two years old.

To sit with a dog on a hillside on a glorious afternoon is to be back in Eden, where doing nothing was not boring—it was peace.

–Milan Kundera

A CURE FOR WHAT AILS YOU

Dogs may be a picture of beauty and strength, but they have their weaknesses, too.

Allergies

Yup, even dogs can have allergies. If your pup is excessively scratching, licking or biting his skin, he may be suffering from an allergic reaction. Common canine allergens include foods such as dairy products, wheat and eggs, as well as environmental triggers, such as pollen, dust and feathers. They can also suffer from contact allergies to substances such as wool or grass. A less common allergen is...yes...human dander. Seems only fair, really...

Parasites

Fleas—Some people cannot think of dogs without thinking of fleas. Fleas are one of a dog's most common aggravations, as witnessed by the plethora of anti-flea powders, soaps, sprays, pills and collars available on the market. While most dogs experience only minor irritation from fleabites, some dogs are actually allergic to the flea's saliva and suffer from severe itching, inflammation and even fur loss when they are bitten.

Ticks—Ticks pose a greater threat to dogs than fleas do, because ticks carry diseases that can be passed on to your pooch. Removing ticks can be a tricky process—the critters dig so deeply into the flesh that the head can break off and stay embedded when the rest of the body is removed. To remove them completely, use tweezers to grab the tick as close to the head as possible and pull it straight out.

Intestinal Parasites

Hookworms—Puppies are especially prone to getting hookworms, which can be passed to them through their mother's milk while they are nursing. Puppies with hookworms quickly become anemic.

Roundworms—These parasites are also common in puppies and young dogs. A dog with roundworms usually has a potbelly and can suffer from a variety of other symptoms, such as pneumonia, diarrhea, dehydration and vomiting.

Tapeworms—To get tapeworms, a dog must swallow fleas bearing tapeworm larvae. Dogs infected with tapeworms often show no symptoms, so the parasites can live undetected in a dog's body for years.

Heartworm—If left untreated or diagnosed too late, heartworm is fatal to dogs. To become infected with heartworm, a dog must be bitten by a mosquito that carries heartworm larvae.

The larvae make their way into the dog's chest and abdominal muscles, eventually moving into the bloodstream. The adult worms settle in the dog's heart, eventually causing congestive heart failure. Symptoms of heartworm include a cough and shortness of breath.

Diseases

Cancer—The types of cancer most commonly seen in the canine population are skin cancer, mammary cancer, lymphoma and bone cancer. As with human cancers, treatment options include surgery, radiation and chemotherapy. Gene therapies may be available in the future, but they are still in the research stages.

Canine Distemper—Canine distemper is an incurable, often fatal disease that was once one of the leading causes of domestic dog mortality. It is contagious and is transmitted by an airborne virus. Dogs are now routinely vaccinated against the disease, so incidences of distemper are far less common than they used to be. Symptoms to watch for include fever, diarrhea, vomiting and a runny nose. More than half of dogs diagnosed with distemper die within the first few weeks of contracting the disease, and many others are euthanized because of the severity of their symptoms.

Kennel Cough—Formally known as tracheobronchitis, kennel cough is a highly contagious disease that is spread by airborne bacteria and viruses. It is similar to a bad cold in humans. Symptoms include a dry, hacking cough, snorting and sneezing. In an otherwise healthy animal, kennel cough usually runs its course within a few weeks, but in dogs with weak immune systems, the disease can develop into a more serious condition, such as pneumonia.

Periodontal Disease—Vets cannot stress enough the importance of keeping Fluffy's mouth clean and fresh. One of the leading causes of illness among canines is oral disease. Unhealthy teeth and gums lead to periodontal disease, which in turn can lead to heart, liver or kidney damage. Oral diseases are largely preventable. All you need is a doggie toothbrush, some doggie toothpaste, quick reflexes and a high pain threshold. Just kidding. Some dogs react pretty well to having their teeth brushed, and those that don't—well, that's what the friendly neighborhood vet is for.

Physical Ailments

Hip Dysplasia—Basically a fancy term for "loose hip joint," hip dysplasia is a degenerative disease that can range in severity from a case of mild discomfort to lameness in the affected limb. A hereditary condition, it can be aggravated by environmental factors, such as poor nutrition and lack of physical activity. Some breeders also suggest that puppies reared on slippery surfaces, such as wooden or concrete floors, are more prone to hip difficulties. Breeds predisposed to hip dysplasia include German shepherds, mastiffs and retrievers.

Limber Tail—What was once known as coldwater tail, limp tail, broken wag or broken tail now goes by the name of limber tail syndrome. The condition is relatively common in sporting dogs, especially hunting dogs, and is a result of strained tail muscles. If your pup's tail hangs limply and is sensitive to the touch, he may be suffering from limber tail. Symptoms can linger for up to a few weeks. The three most common causes for limber tail are exposure to wet, cold weather, overexertion and being confined in a crate for an extended period.

Common Injuries

It's Getting Hot in Here—Summer and dogs in parked cars do not mix. Even when a window is cracked, the temperature inside the car can soar to almost 120°F (50°C). In that kind of heat, all the panting in the world isn't going to bring your pooch's body temperature down to a safe level. It can take less than 10 minutes for a dog to die from heat stroke.

Hangin' Out—The next time you and your pooch take a little Sunday drive, you might want to keep your windows rolled up, so he can't hang his head out. Although it seems an innocent enough activity (and he looks so darned cute with his ears flapping in the wind), a dog can be seriously injured while dangling his head out the window, if road debris or insects fly into his eyes or ears. At high speeds, getting a fly in the eye can cause Fido some serious discomfort—and even permanent damage.

Naughty Kitty—Some of the most common eye injuries dogs suffer come courtesy of cat paws. Cats' claws are notoriously filthy, and even the slightest scratch on a dog's eye can become infected, sometimes causing lasting damage, if left untreated.

Give a Dog a Bone?—Did Old Mother Hubbard get it wrong? The jury is still out on whether or not people should be tossing bones to little Fluffy. Some suggest that bones are potentially hazardous because they splinter and the shards can shred a dog's gums, throat and digestive system. Those who would throw a dog a bone argue that bones are a source of nutrients and help a dog exercise his jaws and keep his teeth clean. Who is right? I'm not sure, but I bet I know which side a dog would stand on…

So Much for "There Are No Bad Foods"—Chocolate, onions, grapes and raisins are toxic to dogs and can be fatal, even in small doses. Better keep your eye on those chocolate-covered raisins!

No Chocolate for You!—The substance in chocolate that makes it poisonous to dogs is called theobromine. If a dog consumes only a small amount, he might just get a little hyperactive, but too much can cause vomiting, tremors, an erratic heartbeat and even death.

> *It's not the size of the dog in the fight;*
> *it's the size of the fight in the dog.*
>
> –Mark Twain

RECORD-BREAKING PUPS

I'm sure all dog owners believe their dogs are winners in some way—cutest, smartest, most charismatic—but some pups have the credentials to back up their owners' claims.

Barely There

The smallest dog on record was a matchbox-sized Yorkshire terrier from England. The petite pup stood only 2.5 inches (6.35 centimeters) tall at the shoulder and measured a mere 3.5 inches (8.90 centimeters) from the tip of its nose to the base of its tail. It weighed 4 ounces (114 grams). The tiny dog lived for less than two years, passing away in 1945.

Itsy Bitsy Puppy

The current record holder for the smallest dog living is Heaven Sent Brandy, a female Chihuahua from Florida. When she set the record in January 2005, she measured a measly 5.9 inches (15.2 centimeters) from her nose to the tip of her tail.

Zorba the Great

The record holder for world's heaviest and world's longest dog is Zorba, an Old English mastiff. When he set the record in 1989, Zorba measured 37 inches (94 centimeters) at the shoulder and 98.8 inches (251 centimeters) from nose to tail. He weighed 315 pounds (143 kilograms)!

Everybody loves a cocker spaniel's ears—except perhaps the spaniel itself. Because the ears are long and dangly, they trap moisture in the ear canal, which can lead to infections.

He's a Whopper!

As of 2007, Gibson, a Great Dane from California, was still hanging onto the record for tallest dog living. He nabbed the title in August 2004, when he measured a towering 42 inches (107 centimeters), taller than some breeds of pony. When he stands on his hind legs, he reaches a height of more than 83 inches (213 centimeters).

Golden Oldie

An Australian cattle dog by the name of Bluey still holds the record for longest-living dog in history. Born on June 7, 1910, in Victoria, Australia, Bluey lived to the ripe old age of 29 years, five months and seven days, more than doubling the expected life span of his breed. The geriatric pup shuffled into doggie heaven, and the *Guinness Book of World Records*, on November 14, 1939.

The Better to Hear You With, My Dear

Basset hounds are supposed to be the breed with the longest ears. Perhaps someone should have mentioned that to Tigger, a bloodhound from Illinois, whose long, droopy ears have secured him a place in the record books. Tigger's right ear measures 13.7 inches (34.9 centimeters), and his left ear is 13.5 inches (34.2 centimeters) long. He has held the longest ears on a dog title since September 29, 2004.

The Dog Jumped Over the Moon

Well, not quite, but this dog jumped over the 5.5-foot (167.6-centimeter) -high obstacle, which was enough to land her in the *Guinness Book of World Records* for the highest jump by a dog. Cinderella May Holly Grey (Cindy for short), a greyhound from Miami, Florida, cleared the jump at the Purina Dog Chow Incredible Dog Challenge show in Missouri on October 3, 2003.

And Then There Were...24!

In January 2005, a mastiff named Tia broke two world records in one day: one for the largest litter and one for most surviving puppies. The previous largest-litter record, which was set by a fox terrier in June 1944, was 23 puppies, but Tia went one better. The pups were delivered by caesarean section, and four of the 24 died soon after the delivery.

Who Needs Opposable Thumbs?

Augie, a golden retriever from Texas, currently holds the world record for the most tennis balls held in the mouth at one time by a dog. On July 6, 2003, the ambitious pup gathered up and held five regulation-size tennis balls.

No Heat Stroke for Me!

Canadians can be proud of this record holder. Striker, a border collie from Quebec City, set the record for a car window most quickly opened by a dog. It took the canine Houdini only 11.43 seconds to roll down a non-electric car window with his paw. The record has stood since September 1, 2004.

Rub a Dub Dub, 848 Dogs in a Tub

In September 2003, students from the University of Sydney's Veterinary Science Foundation broke the record for the highest number of dogs washed and toweled dry by 12 people in eight hours. The previous record, held by a university group from the Netherlands, was 715 dogs. The Sydney University team bathed 848 dogs in seven hours and 40 minutes, before running out of dirty dogs to wash. I suppose it would have been cheating to roll a few dogs in the dirt and bathe them again.

A BREED OR NOT A BREED?

No one really knows how many domestic dog breeds exist in the world today, because people cannot seem to agree on which dogs should qualify as distinct breeds and which ones are simply variations of the same breed. While some organizations put the number of dog species between 400 and 500, the international organization for dog breeders, the FCI (Federation Cynologique Internationale) or World Canine Organization, recognizes 335 breeds, not including those whose status is pending. Because there are far too many breeds to list them all, I have included only a small sample of breeds for each category.

The FCI's Eleven Breed Groups

- Sheepdogs and Cattle Dogs (except Swiss Cattle Dogs)
- Pinschers, Schnauzers, Molossians, Swiss Mountain Dogs and Swiss Cattle Dogs
- Terriers
- Dachshunds
- Spitzes and Primitive Dogs
- Scent Hounds and Related Breeds
- Pointing Dogs
- Retrievers, Flushing Dogs and Water Dogs
- Companion and Toy Dogs
- Sighthounds
- Provisionally Accepted Breeds

SHEEPDOGS AND CATTLE DOGS (EXCEPT SWISS CATTLE DOGS)

These herding dogs are usually submissive and alert, and are easily trainable.

Australian Cattle Dog

When British colonists settled in Australia, they brought their herding dogs, mostly collies, with them, but the dogs did not adjust well to the harsh Australian climate. In an effort to create a more rugged animal to herd their cattle, the colonists crossed collies with dingoes. However, the new breed was still not quite what the farmers were looking for, so they threw a few Dalmatians and bull terriers into the mix, and a new breed— the Australian cattle dog—was born. This is not a bask-all-day-in-the-sunshine kind of dog. It has strong herding instincts and was bred to work. When this dog isn't given a job to keep it busy, it has been known to start herding the animals that live nearby, whether they're ducks, chickens, rabbits or even people. The Australian cattle dog is also known as the Queensland heeler and the blue heeler.

Border Collie

As far as energy levels are concerned, the border collie puts the Energizer bunny to shame. This herding dog never stops, and its mind is just as active. It is thought to be, if not the smartest dog, at least very high in the running. Because it is just so darned cute, people often assume a border collie makes an ideal pet. But this is a working dog—without a way to burn off energy, it can become neurotic and even destructive. The border collie originated in the border country of England and Scotland,

where it was used to herd sheep. It can single-handedly control an entire flock and is known for the characteristic crouching posture it adopts while herding.

German Shepherd

The German shepherd was originally bred to be a herding dog, but today it is more commonly used as a police dog, guide dog, sniffer dog (especially for detecting narcotics and explosives) and for rescue and recovery work. It originated, not surprisingly, in Germany. The German shepherd was renamed the Alsatian after World War I, so that it would not suffer from anti-German sentiment.

Puli

I like to think of this dog as the Rasta dog, because its long, corded coat looks very much like dreadlocks. Some people have compared the puli, rather less flatteringly, to a giant dustmop. The puli is a highly intelligent dog, right up there with the border collie, and was bred as a herder. It likely originated in India or Tibet.

Rottweiler

This much-maligned dog traces its roots back to the Roman Empire, where its ancestors served as war dogs. However, the Rottweiler as we know it today originated in a village named Rottweil, in Schwaben, Germany, during the 1800s. It was bred as a herding dog but became a top choice for a police dog because of its strength, courage and fiercely protective nature. Poorly trained dogs can be aggressive, which is why this breed has such a bad reputation.

Saarloos Wolfhound

In the 1940s, a Dutch geneticist named Leendert Saarloos crossed a male German shepherd with a female wolf. The resulting dog—the Saarloos wolfhound—not only looks like a wolf but has also retained a lot of wolf-like behaviors. Wary of strangers, it is more comfortable as part of a pack and also has a tendency to pace back and forth, much like its wild cousins.

DOG FACT

Almost one-third of all dog owners have serious problems with their pet because they chose the pooch for its cute little face, instead of researching the breed and taking its characteristics into consideration before making a decision.

PINSCHERS, SCHNAUZERS, MOLOSSIANS, SWISS MOUNTAIN DOGS AND SWISS CATTLE DOGS

The breeds in this category make good watchdogs.

Doberman (Doberman Pinscher)

The Doberman was named for Louis Dobermann, a German tax collector in the mid-19th century, who collected money from people who were sometimes not eager to hand it over. Deciding that he needed a guard dog for protection, Dobermann bred a variety of dogs (the exact species he used are not known—apparently he was a pretty poor record keeper for a tax collector—but likely candidates include the German shepherd, the Rottweiler, the Great Dane and the greyhound) to create an animal with all the qualities he thought a good guard dog should have. The resulting breed is commonly used as a guard dog today.

English Bulldog

The English bulldog originated in Great Britain, where it was primarily used in animal fights, especially bull baiting. This dog was built for strength. Known for its sturdy build, powerful neck and strong jaws, the bulldog was bred to have a lower jaw that is longer than the upper one and a nose that points backwards, so that the dog could still breath with its jaws locked onto a bull's hide. Because of the position of its nose, the bulldog is a world-class snorer.

German Boxer (Boxer)

Another dog of German origin, the boxer was bred as a hunter and was mostly used in packs to take down bears and wild boars. It was not expected to kill the animal it caught; instead, it was trained to pin down its quarry until the human hunters got there and finished off the trapped animal. The boxer was also a popular breed for the dog-fighting ring until the 1860s.

Mastiff

The mastiff, or Old English mastiff, also originated in Great Britain and is believed to be the oldest British breed. It is a descendant of the huge dogs that the Celts and Normans used as canine warriors. In the past, this powerful dog was used for bear-baiting, bull-baiting and even lion-baiting. It would generally face a bull alone but fought in packs against bears and lions. Despite its bloody

past, the mastiff is a sweet-natured, gentle dog that is slow to attack. Even as a guard dog, it is more likely to corner an intruder than attack.

Newfoundland Dog

This gentle giant is the quintessential waterdog. It has a thick undercoat to trap heat, an oily outer coat to repel water and webbed feet. It also uses its tail as a rudder when it swims. And it loves to swim. If you stand between a Newf and water, you'd better be prepared to get wet. As the name suggests, this breed originated in Newfoundland. One theory for its origin suggests that early fishermen from England brought their dogs with them, and when the men returned to Europe for the winter months, they left the dogs behind to fend for themselves. When the dogs couldn't find enough food on land, they took to the sea, gradually evolving into the Newfoundland dog as we know it today. This breed was known as the bear dog and the Greater St. John's dog in the early 18th century but has been called the Newfoundland dog since 1775.

Saint Bernard

Named for Bernard de Menthon, an Augustine monk who founded a hospice for weary travelers in the Alps, the Saint Bernard is one of the most famous rescue dogs. By the mid-18th century, this breed was already slogging its way through deep snow to find and dig out people trapped by avalanches. The canteen of brandy is most likely just a myth, though.

TERRIERS

*These dogs are very independent and were originally
bred for hunting animals in burrows.*

Airedale Terrier

What do you get if you cross an otterhound, a bull terrier, a
Gordon setter and a black and tan collie? Why, an Airedale terrier, of course! Largest of the terriers, the Airedale was bred to be
an all-purpose kind of dog—hunter, retriever and guard dog, all
rolled into one. The breed originated in Yorkshire, England, in
the dale of the River Aire, so you can see where it gets its name.

Kerry Blue Terrier
A good pet choice for dog lovers who don't want dog hair coating
everything in the house, the Kerry blue terrier doesn't shed; its
coat is more like human hair than typical dog fur. Unfortunately,
the time saved on vacuuming will probably be spent on coat
maintenance with this breed, because its coat never stops growing
and needs regular brushing and trimming. The Kerry blue originated in Ireland and was used to hunt "vermin," such as rats, rabbits and foxes. This feisty pup was also used in the dog-fighting
ring and could even hold its own against a badger, a notoriously
fierce animal. Today, this terrier is used as a police dog in Ireland.

Jack Russell Terrier

This confident little terrier doesn't seem to realize how small it
is. It has the heart of a Rottweiler crammed into an itty-bitty
package. Originally bred in England to hunt foxes in their dens,
this little pooch had to be fearless to take on its quarry in the
confines of an underground burrow. And fearless it is. The Jack
Russell won't think twice about taking on a dog much larger
than itself, and it will even try to get the upper hand with its
human owner.

Skye Terrier

This longhaired pooch, believed to be the oldest Scottish terrier, originated on the Isle of Skye in the Scottish Hebrides. One theory of origin for this breed suggests that a group of Maltese dogs swam ashore from a 16th-century shipwreck and bred with terriers native to the island, creating the Skye terrier. This breed was originally used to hunt otters, foxes and badgers by locating them in their dens and digging them out. It eventually became a favorite of the English and Scottish courts.

DACHSHUNDS

*This breed was also bred for flushing
or hunting prey in burrows.*

Although it is thought to be descended from dogs that date back to ancient Egypt, the modern day dachshund originated in Germany. It was bred to hunt badgers, and its name is German for "badger dog." The dachshund's extremely long body and stubby legs made it possible for the dog to chase animals in their underground burrows. Its curved tail not only helped the dog's owner follow the pooch while it was tracking an animal in tall grass, it gave the owner something to tug on, should the dog get stuck in a burrow while pursuing its quarry. Unfortunately, the unnatural length of this dog's body also makes the dachshund prone to spinal problems.

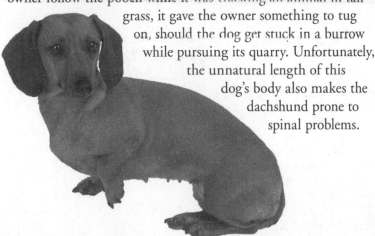

SPITZES AND PRIMITIVE DOGS

These breeds are excellent hunting dogs and watchdogs. Among the oldest breeds of domestic dogs, they have changed little in form and behavior from their wolf ancestors.

Akita Inu

Akita-type dogs date back at least 5000 years in Japan. The Akita gets its name from the Akita prefecture, where it is believed to have originated. The Akita's ancestors were bred for bear hunting and dog fighting, so they were encouraged to be extremely aggressive. This aggressive tendency is still visible in the Akita's reaction to animals that do not recognize its dominance.

Basenji

Another ancient breed, the Basenji has been around for at least 4000 years and was kept as a hunting dog by the pharaohs of ancient Egypt. This unique dog yodels instead of barking, is completely odorless and grooms itself like a cat, licking its paw and then passing the damp paw over its fur.

Canaan Dog

Named for the land in which it originated (now Israel), the Canaan dog is one of the world's oldest breeds. Drawings of dogs that resemble the Canaan have been found in tombs that date back to 2200 BC. This breed makes an excellent guard dog and is kept by Bedouins to herd and protect their sheep. Although it is gentle with people, the Canaan is extremely aggressive with other dogs; even the puppies have to be kept separate from each other, because they just can't seem to get along.

DID YOU  KNOW?

Spitzes are believed to be the oldest breed of domestic dog.

Chow Chow

It may look like a big, fuzzy plush toy, but the chow chow was bred to hunt, and it is known as a stubborn, dominant breed. This dog originated in China and is thought to date back to 150 BC. Two unique characteristics for the chow chow are its

black tongue and its back legs, which are almost straight and give the dog a rather stilted gait. Its Chinese name, *Songshi Quan*, translates to mean "puffy-lion dog."

Xoloitzcuintle

Also known as the Mexican hairless, this strange-looking creature dates back more than 3000 years. Although the Aztecs believed the xoloitzcuintle (or "xolo") was sacred, they also bred the dog to be eaten as a delicacy and sacrificed it to their gods. This breed comes in three sizes: toy, miniature and standard, the last resembling a bald, dark-skinned greyhound.

 DOG FACT The Basenji is the only domestic dog that can't bark. It yodels instead.

I wonder if other dogs think poodles are members of a weird religious cult.

–Rita Rudner

SCENT HOUNDS AND RELATED BREEDS

Dogs in this breed category are used for hunting, often in packs.

Basset Hound

This short-legged dog originated in France, where it was bred to hunt rabbits. Being so close to the ground allowed the basset

hound to maneuver through thick bushes after its quarry. Breeders got a little carried away for a while, selecting traits to give this dog an even more stretched appearance, but they have since regained their sanity and come to realize that stubby legs plus a long back equals bone and joint problems. The basset hound's sense of smell is legendary, second only to that of the bloodhound.

Beagle

Originally bred in Great Britain as a hunting dog, the beagle specialized in tracking hares, but it was also used to hunt pheasants and other game birds, red deer and even bobcats, wild boars and foxes. Today, many beagles are put to work as sniffer dogs, working with border guards to find food in people's luggage.

Bloodhound

The bloodhound is also known as Chien de Saint-Hubert, for a monastery in Belgium where it possibly originated. The breed is thought to be at least 700 years old. This hound has the best sense of smell of any dog. It was bred to track humans, and it can follow trails that are already a few days old. In the U.S., the bloodhound is the only animal whose findings are admissible as evidence in court.

Rhodesian Ridgeback

This is not a dog I would want to confront if I was sneaking onto someone's property under cover of darkness (not that I do things like that...). The ridgeback was bred to be a hunter, and in its native Zimbabwe, it was used to hunt lions. Although it is gentle and loving with people it trusts, it can be aggressive with strangers if not well trained. The "ridgeback" part of this dog's name refers to a line of stiff hairs running along the dog's spine that grow in the opposite direction of the dog's other hairs.

Barking dogs don't bite.

–Chinese proverb

POINTING DOGS

These hunting dogs point to the location of prey, flush out the animal once the hunter is within shooting distance and then retrieve the dead animal.

Irish Setter

This beautiful chestnut-colored dog dates back to the 1700s and is descended from the much older Spanish setter. It was bred to work with hunters who netted game birds, such as pheasant and quail. Once the setter has sniffed out the location of its quarry, the dog "sets," or freezes, alerting the hunter to the bird's presence and giving him time to throw the net over the bird before it flushes.

Magyar Vizsla

Known for its affectionate nature, the Magyar Vizsla is sometimes lovingly called the "Velcro dog," because it likes to stick close to its people. Originating in Hungary, this breed was developed in the 18th century by crossing Turkish hunting dogs (which are now extinct) with pointers and, eventually, German shepherds. Until the end of World War I, owning a Magyar Vizsla was a sign of aristocracy in Hungary.

DOG FACT The Qimmiq, also known as the Canadian Eskimo dog, is the official animal of Nunavut. The breed is one of the oldest purebreeds in the world, dating back at least 4000 years!

Pointer

Also known as an English pointer, this athletic dog was bred to sniff out game birds and is famous for the characteristic pose it uses to point out the location of a hidden bird. The pointing instinct is strong in this breed, and puppies as young as two months old will already adopt the pose. This breed originated in England and dates back to at least the 1600s.

Weimaraner

During the 18th and 19th centuries, a few thrifty individuals decided they needed an all-purpose hunting dog—one that would point and retrieve small quarry and even take down large animals, such as bears and deer—as well as a guard dog. This beautiful, silvery grey dog is the fruit of their labor. These days, the Weimaraner is commonly used as a police or rescue dog.

RETRIEVERS, FLUSHING DOGS AND WATER DOGS

*These breeds find and retrieve game,
especially waterfowl.*

Cocker Spaniel (English Cocker Spaniel)

Although it is usually thought of as a pampered house pet, the cocker spaniel is actually a skilled hunter and retriever of game birds. Instead of pointing to the bird, the cocker flushes it and

drives it toward the hunter, who waits nearby, trusty gun in hand. This dog gets its name from the woodcock, the bird it was originally bred to hunt.

English Springer Spaniel
Like the cocker spaniel, the English springer spaniel is a flushing dog. The breed originated in Great Britain at least 400 years ago and was paired with a falcon for hunting. The dog located and flushed the game bird, and the awaiting falcon swooped in to capture the panicked prey.

Kooikerhondje

Originally bred in the Netherlands to hunt ducks, the Kooikerhondje trembled on the brink of extinction by the end of World War II. The efforts of a woman named Baroness van Hardenbroek van Ammerstol saved the breed. She paid a traveling salesman to keep an eye out for the dogs and started a breeding program with those that were found. Although the Kooikerhondje is today relatively well established in some European nations, it is still largely unknown on this side of the pond.

Labrador Retriever
Another made-in-Canada pooch, the Labrador retriever is one of the most popular and widespread breeds of dog. This water dog originated in Newfoundland and was trained by fishermen to haul their fishing nets to shore. Today, the lab is commonly used as a sniffer dog, a police dog, a guide dog and a search and rescue dog.

Dogs laugh, but they laugh with their tails.

–Max Eastman

COMPANION AND TOY DOGS

These dogs were bred to provide us with a little company.

Bichon Frisé

This pampered pooch has been around for a long time. It appears in paintings that date back to the Middle Ages and, for centuries, acted as a bed warmer for noble families. It is believed to have originated in Spain or Belgium and is a cross between a water spaniel and a poodle. Like the poodle, the bichon does not shed, and its coat must be trimmed to prevent it from becoming an unruly mass of fuzz.

Chihuahua

It's ironic that the smallest dog in the world is named for the largest state of the country in which it originated. This Mexican breed was officially discovered in 1850, but reports of Chihuahua-like dogs date back much farther. This tiny pooch is believed to be a descendant of the Chinese crested. I guess we know who got the looks in that family…

Chinese Crested

This breed of dog is so ugly that it's cute. That may seem a little harsh, but what else can be said of an animal that is mostly pink and grey skin with wispy tufts of fur? Actually, there are two types of Chinese crested—hairless and the less common powderpuff (which looks sort of like a giant, four-legged cotton ball when not groomed). The Chinese crested is known for its even temper and sunny disposition.

Maltese

Another ancient breed, the Maltese is named for the island of Malta, where, in antiquity, it was often used as a barter item. Although it is thought to be a descendant of a breed that was used to hunt rats, the Maltese as we know it today was bred exclusively as a lap dog for royalty.

Poodle

Many people find it hard to take the poodle seriously. It is frequently dismissed as foppish and somewhat ridiculous, no doubt because of the undignified haircut it often sports. But this dog

is actually one of the smartest breeds, and though the miniature and toy varieties are companion pets, the standard poodle was originally bred to hunt. Poodle aficionados cannot agree whether the dog originated in France or Germany, but its name might be of German origin. Some suggest that "poodle" derived from *pudel*, the German word for "to paddle," a reference to the dog's waterfowl hunting past.

DID YOU  KNOW?

The best-named dog out there has got to be the Labradoodle. Say it with me…Labradoodle. Brings a smile to your face, doesn't it? Even if this dog wasn't cute and fuzzy, I would love it for its name alone. The Labradoodle is, as you might have guessed, a cross between a Labrador retriever and a standard poodle. Although it is not recognized as a breed by any official dog organization, it is gaining popularity with dog lovers, probably because its name is just so darned fun to say. Labradoodle, Labradoodle, Labradoodle….

Shih Tzu

The Shih Tzu is a descendant of the Shi-Tze-kou, or "Tibetan lion-dog," which reportedly guarded Buddhist temples. In the 17th century, the Shi-Tze-kou was taken to the imperial palace in China and bred with the Pekinese, and possibly the Lhasa Apso, resulting in the Shih Tzu as we know it today. This little pooch became so highly regarded in China that, until the 1930s, it was forbidden to trade, sell or give the dog to anyone outside of the country.

SIGHTHOUNDS

The oldest form of hunting dog, sighthounds were bred for speed. They track their prey by sight, rather than by scent. Once they spot their quarry, they pursue it and capture it by running it down and overpowering it.

Greyhound

Greyhounds were once the "in" dog of royal families and can be seen in many royal portraits, sitting patiently beside their owners. The dogs were bred as hunters and were highly prized for their speed. Today, they are mostly known as racing dogs, reaching speeds of up to 44 miles (70 kilometers) per hour. These dogs love to run and will chase anything that moves. They just can't help themselves. Surprisingly, pet greyhounds are notoriously lazy when they are indoors with the family, preferring to lounge around and soak up the affection they know they deserve.

Irish Wolfhound

The largest and strongest of all dog breeds, this massive dog can grow as large as a small pony. The Celts used wolfhounds as war dogs, training the animals to drag men out of chariots or from the backs of horses. In Ireland, the wolfhound was greatly sought after for its hunting skills and was used to take down elk and wolves. Despite its bloody past, the wolfhound is actually a gentle animal.

DOG FACT

Dalmatian puppies are white when they are born and get their characteristic spots as they grow older.

Saluki

Named for an ancient Arabian city, the Saluki breed originated in the Middle East. Egyptian pharaohs kept these dogs as hunters, and mummified dogs have been uncovered in tombs alongside their mummified royal owners. Saluki remains have also been discovered at a site in Iraq that dates back to the Sumerian Empire.

Whippet

A cross between a terrier and a greyhound, the whippet originated in Great Britain, where it served as the common folk's racing dog. This sweet-natured creature is very sensitive, both physically and emotionally. It cannot take cold weather and does not like to be left alone. A whippet is happiest when it is running or when it is curled up on the couch next to its owner.

If a dog will not come to you after having looked you in the face, you should go home and examine your conscience.

–Woodrow Wilson

PROVISIONALLY ACCEPTED BREEDS

This category includes dogs that the FCI has decided meet the requirements to be recognized as a breed but that have not yet received that status.

Australian Shepherd

Despite its name, the Australian shepherd actually originated in California. This breed was developed from dogs that were imported into the U.S. with Australian sheep. Although it was bred to be a herding dog, the Australian shepherd is often used as a guide dog, a police dog and in search and rescue. In the 1950s, it was even trained to perform in rodeos.

White Swiss Shepherd (Berger Blanc Suisse)
Also known as the Berger Blanc Suisse, the White Swiss shepherd is a white variant of the German shepherd. Popular in Germany and Switzerland, it is said to be a kinder, gentler version of its more colorful cousin. The White Swiss shepherd makes an excellent guide dog and is used heavily in search and rescue. Many police forces will not use this breed because its white coat shows up too well at night, making it an easy target.

A dog owns nothing, yet is seldom dissatisfied.
–Irish proverb

UNRECOGNIZED BREEDS

Because the dogs in this category are not purebred, as defined by the FCI, the organization does not officially recognize them as breeds. However, they are easily as intelligent as purebreds and are not as prone to the same genetic problems, because their genetic material is more diverse. Some of these breeds are recognized as purebred by other organizations.

In addition to the Turkish breeds listed below, other unrecognized breeds include the Italian mountain dog (also known as the Alp mastiff), the Boerboel, the Northern Inuit dog and the Mudhol hound.

Akbash

The Akbash is an ancient breed that dates back at least 3000 years. It originated in Turkey, perhaps in the region west of Ankara, where it is still commonly used to guard livestock. The Akbash's coat is pure white, and it has been suggested that all white herding dogs in Europe descended from this breed. It's also thought that early Turkish farmers bred the dog to have a white coat, so that they could tell at a glance whether the animal mixing with their flock was the guard dog at work or a wolf stalking the sheep.

Kangal

Dog lovers in Turkey must shake their heads in dismay when reminded that their national dog is not recognized internationally as an official breed. In its native land, this dog is widely popular as a guardian for livestock. Kangals are thought to have originated in the Sivas province of Turkey, and only those born in the area of Sivas are considered purebreds. Kangal-type dogs not born around the city of Sivas are referred to as Karabash dogs. All purebreds must be recorded in the Kangal registry.

REAL DOGS

Some dogs have taken their role as "man's best friend" to the extreme, dedicating themselves to the people in their lives and, in some cases, even dying for them.

Don't Move, Or I'll Bite

In the 1989 film *K-9*, Koton starred as Jerry Lee, a drug-sniffing dog with attitude that helps James Belushi's character uncover a drug smuggling ring. Outside of the movies, Koton was a K-9 officer in the Kansas City, Missouri, police force. He was shot and killed in the line of duty in 1991, while chasing a suspect wanted for the murder of another police officer.

A Guiding Paw

The first formally trained guide dog in the U.S. was a female German shepherd by the name of Buddy. Her owner, Morris Frank, was one of the founders of The Seeing Eye, the first guide dog school in United States. Although people tend to use the term "seeing eye dog" to refer to any dog that acts as a guide for the blind, this term correctly applies only to canines trained by The Seeing Eye; dogs trained by other schools are referred to as "guide dogs." Trained in Switzerland by Dorothy Harrison Eustis, Buddy graduated on April 25, 1928, and returned to the U.S. with Frank, working at his side as he trained other dogs with the methods he learned from Eustis in Switzerland. A 1984 made-for-TV movie, *Love Leads the Way: A True Story*, explores the relationship between Morris Frank and Buddy and tells the story of Frank's battle to get legal recognition for guide dogs, so they could be allowed on buses and in public buildings, from which pet dogs were banned.

A Race for the Cure

Balto, a Siberian husky sled dog, mushed his way to fame on February 2, 1925, when he led his team, which was carrying a much-needed diphtheria serum, through a whiteout into Nome, Alaska. Gunnar Kaasen's team, led by Balto, was one of more than 20 dog sled teams that took part in "the Great Race of Mercy," a relay assembled to deliver the medication from Nenana to Nome to combat a looming diphtheria epidemic. The relay lasted five-and-a-half days and covered 674 miles (1085 kilometers). Mushing teams ran around the clock through blizzard conditions and temperatures that dropped to –55°F (–53°C) and lower, with the windchill. Balto's team was meant to run only the second-last leg of the relay, but, as Balto navigated through screaming winds and driving snow, he and his team missed the last dog sled team and had to complete the journey themselves. Klassen and his dogs arrived in Nome to a hero's welcome and international acclaim.

The dogs toured the U.S. as part of a vaudeville show until 1927, when they were purchased by the residents of Cleveland, Ohio, and housed in the Cleveland Zoo. Balto passed away in March 1933. A statue of his likeness stands in New York City's Central Park, and his stuffed body is on display in the Cleveland Museum of Natural History.

Uncommon Valor
Gander, a Newfoundland dog, accompanied Canadian troops to Hong Kong in 1941 to fight the Japanese. He warned his troops if the enemy was nearby and attacked Japanese soldiers that came too close to his battalion. When an enemy grenade was lobbed into his battalion's camp, Gander picked it up and carried it away from the soldiers. It exploded in his mouth, killing him instantly. For his bravery, Gander was awarded the Dickin Medal, the canine equivalent of the Victoria Cross. He is the only Canadian dog to receive this medal.

Now, That's What I Call Loyalty

Even after John Gray passed away in 1858 and was buried in Greyfriars churchyard in Scotland, his Skye terrier, Bobby, stayed by his side. Or at least as close to Gray's side as he could get. The little terrier lay beside his owner's grave, only leaving it once a day to get food from the neighborhood inn at which he and John had lunched together every day. Greyfriars Bobby, as he came to be known, kept up his vigil for 14 years, until his death in 1872. The townsfolk erected a statue in honor of the devoted pup, and it still stands at the cemetery gate today.

The Canary Islands were not named after the little yellow bird we all know and love but for a large breed of dog that was found there. The islands' Latin name was *Canariae insulae*, which translates as "island of dogs."

Cloning Around

First, there was Dolly, the first cloned sheep; now we have Snuppy, the first cloned dog. Born in April 2005, Snuppy is the result of a cell that was taken from the ear of a male Afghan hound named Tei, injected into an empty egg cell and implanted into a female yellow Labrador retriever. He is the work of a team of scientists from Seoul National University, which is why he has that rather unfortunate name (a meshing of SNU and "puppy").

Yo Quiero Fame and Fortune

You may not know her by name, but you would definitely recognize this little pooch if you saw her, or any of her paraphernalia. Part of a Taco Bell ad campaign launched in 1997, Gidgit, the "talking" Chihuahua (comedian Carlos Alazraqui did the voiceover) became famous for her tagline, "*Yo quiero* Taco Bell." T-shirts, posters and even bobble-head figures of the dog flew off the shelves during the height of the campaign's popularity. Taco Bell dropped the Chihuahua campaign in 2000, and Gidgit fell out of the limelight, though she did continue acting. She was last seen in the role of Bruiser's mother in *Legally Blonde 2*.

He's a She!

Spuds McKenzie was huge in the late 1980s. The brainchild of the marketing department at Anheuser-Busch Company, suppliers of Bud Light beer, Spuds was a white bull terrier with a black patch around one eye. He was featured in loads of commercials and on billboards, always surrounded by beautiful women and either partying or performing sporty, but un-doglike, activities, such as waterskiing. Spuds paraphernalia, including T-shirts, mugs and stuffed animals, soon popped up everywhere. The party-loving pooch was involved in a bit of a scandal, however, when it was discovered that the dog portraying Spuds was actually female. Her real name was Honey Tree Evil Eye. She died in May 1993 from kidney failure.

Just Call Me Handsome

Handsome Dan, a feisty little bulldog, has been the mascot for Yale's athletic teams since 1889. The mascot has two forms: a person dressed in a silly bulldog costume (as you would expect for a college mascot) and a real, live bulldog. Yale's current bulldog is obviously not the same pooch that first held the position; in fact, he is the 16th. The title of "Handsome Dan" is passed from dog to dog, as the mascot of the day steps down or passes away.

Step Aside, Yuri

The title of first astronaut should actually go to a stray dog named Laika. On November 3, 1957, Laika was a passenger on the Soviet satellite *Sputnik 2*, making her the first living creature to enter Earth's orbit. Things did not end well for the Russian pup, however. Because her craft had no recovery system, Soviet scientists intended to euthanize Laika a few days into her adventure, once they had studied the effects of space travel on her body. Sadly, she died a few hours after the launch, probably from overheating and stress.

In the Eye of the Beholder

Beautiful Joe, as he came to be known, was anything but beautiful after his owner was finished with him. The abusive man beat the young terrier almost to death, then cut off his ears and tail. Rescued by a man named Walter Moore, the mistreated dog was nursed back to health by Moore's daughter, Louise. The pup's plight so moved Margaret (Marshall) Saunders that she wrote a fictionalized version of the story, which was published in 1894. The novel, titled *Beautiful Joe*, tells the story of its namesake through the eyes of the abused pooch. It went on to become a bestseller and was the first Canadian book to sell more than a million copies. In 1963, a park was named in his honor in Beautiful Joe's hometown of Meaford, Ontario.

DID YOU KNOW?

The "Martha" in the Beatles' song "Martha My Dear" is Paul McCartney's pet sheepdog.

I'm Sure He Has a Winning Personality

It must be true that a mother's love is blind. Karen Quigley, owner of a Chinese crested/Chihuahua mix named Elwood, describes her pup as "the cutest thing that ever lived." Apparently, not everyone agrees. In fact, after placing second in the 2006 World's Ugliest Dog Contest, little Elwood went on to out-ugly all other contestants in 2007, taking home first prize. Mostly bald, with dark skin and a bushy patch of white fur on his head,

Elwood has huge, googly eyes and a tongue that perpetually lolls out of the side of his mouth. Those who have seen him suggest that he looks rather like a canine version of Yoda or ET, so you can just imagine what a handsome devil he is. Quigley saved the homely hound from an early entrance to the Big Doggy Park in the Sky when he was just a pup—his breeder was going to put him down because she thought he was too ugly to sell.

The Philosopher Dog

Not content to lounge in the shadow of her owner, bestselling author Dean Koontz, Trixie Koontz, the golden retriever (or as she would say, "Trixie, who is dog") penned her own book, *Life is Good: Lessons in Joyful Living*. And this wasn't the philosophical pooch's only foray into writing—she is also credited as the author of *Christmas is Good: Trixie Treats and Holiday Wisdom*. Trixie, described as an "essayist and literary critic," also has her

own column on Dean Koontz's official website. In her early years, the multi-talented pooch worked with wheelchair-bound people as a service dog for Canine Companions for Independence, and all proceeds from her two books are donated to that organiza-tion. Trixie passed away in June 2007 (though she still writes the column, "from the other side"). In remembrance, I will share with you a shining example of her philosophy, taken from her first book:

Share your heart, and lonely path becomes happy parade. Sounds like cheesy greeting card, but is true. Which reminds me: cheese. Don't just stop along path to smell roses. Stop for cheese sometimes. More cheese than roses. No bees in cheese.

Can't argue with that...

BEHIND EVERY GREAT PERSON IS A GREAT DOG

Many famous folks throughout the ages have enjoyed the company of dogs, just like the rest of us do.

Politically Savvy Pooch

Prime Minister William Lyon Mackenzie King, Canada's longest-serving prime minister, was also possibly the most eccentric. Known as a bit of a loner, King preferred the company of his Irish terrier, Pat, to that of most people. King named all of his dogs Pat, but he was closest to the original Pat, given to him as a gift in 1924. The terrier lived to the ripe old age of 17, passing away in July 1941. In one of King's speeches, recorded in 1944, the Prime Minister credits his "little friend Pat" with teaching him about honor and fidelity. King's diaries, which were released after his death, revealed that he often used a Ouija board or crystal ball to communicate with his dead dog on matters of national policy.

Climate Change Canine

Stéphane Dion has a Siberian husky named Kyoto, which he named for the Kyoto Protocol. He and his family purchased the pooch to boost their spirits after the Liberals were booted from power in January 2006. Dion says he chose an Arctic breed and named the dog after the protocol as an expression of his concern about what the new Conservative government would do to combat climate change.

DID YOU KNOW?

In 1814, while sneaking away from his exile on the island of Elba, Napoleon was washed overboard. The ship's Newfoundland dog jumped into the sea and dragged him to safety, allowing Napoleon to continue on to France and regain control of the government.

Don't Drop the Dog

U.S. President George W. Bush made headlines in August 2003, when he lost his grip on his Scottish terrier, Barney, and dropped the pooch onto the tarmac of the Texas State Technical College Airport in Waco, Texas. Captured on film, the event is probably far from the photo op the President was hoping for. In the photo, members of the Waco Midway Little League Softball World Series championship team look on in shock, as poor little Barney lands on his furry back on the pavement. The presidential pooch was apparently not injured by the fall, but I'm not sure the same can be said about the President's reputation. He was flayed in the media for his clumsiness.

Beazley Who?

Barney is not the only pup to share the White House with the Commander-in-Chief and the First Lady. Miss Beazley, also a Scottish terrier, became a member of the Bush household in 2005, when the President bought her as a birthday gift for his wife. Little Beazley Weazley, as she is affectionately known, has been totally eclipsed by big brother Barney in the fame department. Whereas Barney has to date starred in nine Barney-cam videos and has several websites dedicated to him, Miss Beazley has appeared in only five videos—always in a bit part. Maybe she's a Democrat...

DID YOU KNOW?

Pablo Picasso was a dog lover and owned several Afghan hounds, a Dalmatian and an Ibizan hound.

He Must be a Leo...
In December 1997, a three-month-old chocolate Labrador retriever became part of the First Family. Given as a gift to U.S. President Bill Clinton, the pup was named Buddy in honor of Clinton's great-uncle, Henry "Buddy" Grisham, who had passed away in summer of that year. Buddy quickly earned the title of "most-photographed presidential pet" and was often seen accompanying the Commander-in-Chief as he traveled the country on presidential business. But Buddy didn't just share Bill Clinton's limelight; the energetic pup often earned his own place in the daily newspapers. He once devoured the contents of a box of doughnuts intended for reporters, and his less-than-loving relationship with Socks, the Clinton cat, was well publicized. Sadly,

in 2002, Buddy made headlines one last time, when he was struck and killed by a car near the Clinton's home in Chappaqua, New York.

No More Food for Fala

Although he was widely known as Fala, U.S. President Franklin D. Roosevelt's Scottish terrier had the rather cumbersome name of Murray the Outlaw of Falahill. Franklin chose the name in honor of one of his Scottish ancestors. Given to Roosevelt as a gift from his cousin, pooch and president quickly became inseparable. Fala slept in his own specially made chair at the foot of Roosevelt's bed, and he and his owner ate their meals together. A bone for Fala was even brought up every morning on Roosevelt's breakfast tray. The White House staff was under strict instructions that no one but the President himself was allowed to feed Fala. Apparently, the engaging little creature was so well liked by staff members that that he was surreptitiously being fed food scraps, and at one point the overstuffed pooch had to be rushed to the hospital, suffering from digestive issues. Fala was also popular with the general public and even had his own secretary to respond to the flood of letters he received from his fans. A statue of Fala stands at the FDR Memorial in Washington, DC.

Fala the Furious

Fala gained national notoriety during the 1944 election campaign, when Republican politicians accused Roosevelt of using taxpayer dollars to send a destroyer to the Aleutian Islands to find the pup, which had supposedly been accidentally left behind. In an address to the Teamsters Union on September 23, 1944, Roosevelt denied the claims, giving a speech that became known as "The Fala Speech." In his address, Roosevelt said that, although he and his family did not resent political attacks on them, Fala did resent the attacks and "...his Scotch soul was furious. He has not been the same dog since."

Third Reich Pup

Although he clearly had little regard for the value of human life, it seems Adolph Hitler had a soft spot for German shepherds. He was given a young female German shepherd as a gift in 1941. Named Blondi, she was often seen by his side during his rule of Nazi Germany. When he moved into the safety of the Führerbunker during the fall of Berlin in April 1945, Hitler took Blondi with him. When it became obvious that Berlin would soon be under Soviet control, Hitler ordered his personal doctor to euthanize Blondi, so she would not suffer at the hands of the Soviets. Before taking his own life, he left orders that his remains should be cremated alongside those of Blondi and Eva Braun, his mistress.

DID YOU  KNOW?

Fredrick the Great, Queen Victoria, Catherine the Great and Mary Queen of Scots were all proud owners of Italian greyhounds.

The better I get to know men,
the more I find myself loving dogs.

–Charles de Gaulle

VIPs (VERY IMPORTANT POOCHES)

Here's something for you to ponder. If some of our cultural icons (the movers and the shakers, if you will) had not been influenced by the dogs in their lives, what would our world be like today? I tell you, those pups just do not get the credit they deserve.

Nightingale's First Patient

Florence Nightingale may never have founded modern nursing had she not met a sheepdog named Cap. Cap was a working dog owned by a neighbor of Nightingale's parents. When Cap's leg was injured by a group of neighborhood boys, the dog's distraught owner planned to euthanize the animal because he couldn't afford to feed a dog unable to earn its keep. Nightingale and a local clergyman inspected the dog's injuries, and the clergyman determined that the dog's leg was only badly bruised. He told Nightingale how to treat the injury, and, thanks to her efforts, the dog was soon as good as new. Nightingale took the experience as a sign that God wanted her to dedicate her life to healing others. The rest, as they say, is history.

The Heart of a Lion

The fifth Dalai Lama, Ngag-dbang-rgya-mtsho, owed his life to his pet Lhasa Apsos. While the Dalai Lama was trying to form an alliance with the Mongols, a move that was not universally popular, a group of assassins crept into his summer palace in Lhasa with the intent of finishing him off. They killed the soldiers guarding the palace's exterior, then snuck inside to find the Dalai Lama's chambers. They hadn't gotten far before the Dalai Lama's Lhasa Apsos began to bark, alerting his personal guards to the impending danger. The guards quickly took care of the assassins, while the Dalai Lama slept safely on. Okay, I don't actually know about the "slept on" part, but it is true that he was kept safe, thanks to the actions of his little pups. The Tibetans commemorated the pooches' bravery by naming their breed *abso seng kye*, meaning "barking lion sentinel dog."

Would You Like a Napkin?

You can't make it through an introductory psychology class without learning about Pavlov and his drooling dogs. In the 1890s and early 1900s, Ivan Pavlov, a Russian scientist, conducted a series of experiments with dogs that shaped our understanding of what is now known as classical conditioning. In his experiment, Pavlov rang a bell before giving his dogs their meal. Before long, because they were conditioned to associate the ringing bell with the arrival of food, the dogs would start salivating once they heard the bell, even if no food was offered afterwards. The term "Pavlov's dog" has made its way into popular culture and is used to describe a person who reacts automatically to a situation without giving it any conscious thought.

Poetic Pup

Famed poet Lord Byron so loved his Newfoundland dog, Boatswain, that when the huge animal died of rabies in 1808, Byron buried him at Newstead Abbey and erected a massive marble monument in his honor. The monument's inscription, "Epitaph to a dog" has become one of Byron's best-known poems. It reads:

> *Near this Spot*
> *Are deposited the Remains*
> *Of one who possessed*
> *Beauty without Vanity,*
> *Strength without Insolence,*
> *Courage without Ferocity,*
> *And all the Virtues of Man*
> *Without his Vices.*
> *This praise, which would be unmeaning Flattery*
> *If inscribed over Human Ashes,*
> *Is but a just tribute to the Memory of*
> *"Boatswain," a Dog*
> *who was born at Newfoundland,*
> *May, 1803,*
> *And died at Newstead Abbey*
> *Nov. 18, 1808.*

DID YOU  KNOW?

Chewbacca of *Star Wars* fame owes his existence in large part to George Lucas' Alaskan malamute, Indiana. When creating the "Chewie" character, Lucas used his huge pup as a source of inspiration. Good thing Indiana wasn't a Chinese crested!

Road Trip, Anyone?

In the fall of 1960, John Steinbeck loaded up his pickup, which he had converted into a camper, and set off on a three-month road trip across the U.S. Sharing the bench seat was his trusty standard poodle, Charles le Chien, better known as Charley. The pair covered more than 10,000 miles (16,000 kilometers), traveling from the east coast to the west coast and back again. Steinbeck documented their journey in his book *Travels With Charley: In Search of America*, which made his pet a household name and won the author the Nobel Prize in Literature in 1962. In the book, Steinbeck referred to Charley as his ambassador and credited the pup with persuading the strangers they met in their travels to lower their guard and open up to the writer. Charley passed away in 1961.

Beware of a silent dog and still water.

–Latin proverb

DOGS WITH STAR POWER

Ours is a culture that worships celebrities—and not just the human ones. Doggie starlets sometimes get just as much media attention as their two-legged celebrity owners.

Not Without My Dog

She may not be as notorious as his owner, Don Cherry, but Blue, an English bull terrier, has achieved a measure of success in her own right. Blue was given to Cherry by the members of the Boston Bruins when he was their coach. She became a fixture at his side on CBC's *Hockey Night in Canada* and also appeared in Cherry's *Rock'Em Sock'Em Hockey* videos. Cherry thought so highly of his pooch that, when the publishers of the book Cherry coauthored, *Grapes: A Vintage View of Hockey,* wanted to use a Blue-free photo on the cover, Cherry threatened to cancel the project entirely. According to Cherry, he told the publishers, "If we don't have the cover, we don't have a book, because Blue is going on." Blue passed away in 1989.

Designer Dogs

At one time, the name Tinkerbell summoned images of a tiny, blonde-haired fairy, dressed in a green dress and itty-bitty green slippers. Now the name is more commonly used in reference to a brown-haired Chihuahua—which could also very well be wearing a green dress and itty-bitty green slippers—and which can usually be found tucked under the arm (or in the purse) of Paris Hilton. The heiress adopted her canine companion after seeing the movie *Legally Blonde*, in which Reese Witherspoon's character, Elle, has a tiny Chihuahua companion named Bruiser. The tiny dog trend caught on, and suddenly accessory mini-mutts were popping up in the pockets and handbags of fashionistas across the land. Tinkerbell appeared alongside Paris in *The Simple Life*, the reality show starring Paris and pal Nicole Ritchie, and the tiny pooch is often spotted with her owner at celebrity functions.

So Many Outfits, So Little Time

Many celebrities are known for living lives of excess, but is it possible to take the whole doggie-fashion thing too far? Tori Spelling doesn't seem to think so. She employs a designer to create clothes for her pet, a pug named Mimi Larue. The pooch has such an extensive collection of designer doggie duds that she owns her own closet.

DID YOU KNOW?

On the July 1, 1956 episode of *The Steve Allen Show*, Elvis Presley sang "Hound Dog" to a basset hound named Sherlock.

Little Dog Duds

One of the more famous celebrity pups has to be Hilary Duff's beloved Little Dog. After all, the dog has an entire line of pet accessories named for her. The Duffs found the pooch, a fox terrier/Chihuahua mix, wandering down a street; when no one came forward to claim her, she was christened Little Dog and adopted into the Duff family. In interviews dating back to her *Lizzie McGuire* days, Hilary often gushes about the pooch, which passed away in 2004, before the launch of the pet accessory line that bears her name. In honor of her pet, Hilary pledged to donate the proceeds from the Little Dog Duff line to support no-kill animal shelters and spay and neuter programs.

Where's the Beef?

Alicia Silverstone has never bought a canine companion from a breeder. Each of her dogs is a rescue dog. Samson, the first pooch Silverstone adopted, was an injured stray that she found wandering the streets of Los Angeles. She has since adopted five more unwanted mutts: Lacey, Scottie, Jeffrey, Cale and Baby. Alicia is a strict vegan and feeds her pups a vegan diet, as well.

Some days you're the dog, some days you're the hydrant.

–Author Unknown

PUPS IN PRINT

Dogs are such a huge part of our everyday lives that it is only natural to find our four-legged friends featured in the pages of books and newspapers.

Comic Canines

☛ Fred Basset (1963–present)—Fred is a short-tempered basset hound, who stars in the British comic strip of the same name, along with an assortment of canine companions, including Jock, a black Scottish terrier, Fifi the poodle and Yorky the Yorkshire terrier. Created by Alex Graham, the strip is unique in that it often doesn't have a punch line. Since Graham's death in 1991, his daughter, Arran, has been penning the strip. For a short while in the mid-1970s, *Fred Basset* enjoyed a little TV exposure, when the strip was turned into a five-minute cartoon that aired on the BBC.

☛ Grimm, *Mother Goose and Grimm* (1984–present)—Grimm is a garbage-loving, car-chasing, cat-tormenting bull terrier that lives in a large shoe with his owner, Mother Goose, and her cat, Attila. The award-winning strip, created by Mike Peters, is syndicated in newspapers worldwide and consistently places in the top 10 for most popular cartoons. It follows Grimm as he wreaks havoc in his fairytale community, and popular fairytale characters often make guest appearances. *Mother Goose and Grimm* has been published in book form and was even turned into a TV show called *Grimmy*.

☛ DJ Dog, *Housebroken* (2003–present)—A former rapper pit bull, DJ Dog (a.k.a. The Notorious D.O.G) has lost his fortune and must now live in suburbia with his attorney's middle class family—but that doesn't mean he can't keep his "street cred." This is the premise of *Housebroken*. The strip is written by Steve Watkins, who himself has a degree in law, and at times it has a definite political bent. Two compilation books have been published, so far, including the enticingly titled *Gangsta Yoga with DJ Dog*.

☛ Little Dog, *Little Dog Lost* (March 2007–present)—Created by Steve Boreman, this newcomer to the newspaper pages follows the adventures of Little Dog as he tries to find his way back home. Along the way, Little Dog meets a variety of characters, including Vernon the turtle and a hungry vulture that tries to talk the pooch into making unwise (read "potentially fatal") decisions. The comic has environmental undertones, commenting on the effect that humans have on the environment, but in a light-hearted way.

☛ Marmaduke (1954–present)—Marmaduke, the famous Great Dane, has been a presence on the comic pages for more than 50 years. Created by Brad Anderson, the strip is currently published in more than 20 countries, including Italy, Germany, Sweden and Norway. It deals with the every-day lives of the Winslow family and their great big dog, who seems to think he is just one of the humans and has a knack for getting himself into trouble.

☞ Odie, *Garfield* (1978–present)—He may not be clever, but he sure is cute. Odie, a yellow beagle and lovable sidekick, spends much of his time panting, drooling and suffering some sort of indignity at the paws of Garfield, the famous lasagna-loving cat. Odie was originally brought into the Arbuckle household by Jon Arbuckle's roommate, and much to Garfield's initial disgust, the dog never left. *Garfield* holds the Guinness World Record for the most widely syndi-cated comic strip—it is published in more than 2700 news-papers worldwide. The strip has also been turned into several animated TV specials, as well as two live-action films.

☞ Snoopy, *Peanuts* (1950–2000)—Another famous beagle—perhaps the *most* famous beagle—is Snoopy, of *Peanuts* fame. When he is not trying to steal Linus' blanket, this lovable pooch can most often be found lying on top of his doghouse, daydreaming. He enjoys more respect and greater popularity than his owner, Charlie Brown, who he always calls "that round-headed kid." *Peanuts* was first published in 1950; the final strip hit newspaper pages on February 13, 2000, one day after Charles Schultz passed away from colon cancer. Snoopy's popularity grew to the point where it could not be contained in the comic strip. He and Charlie Brown were adopted as semi-official mascots for NASA's *Apollo 10* mission.

Children aren't dogs; adults aren't gods.

–Haitian proverb

CANINE CLASSICS

Curling up with a classic book is like getting reacquainted with a bunch of old friends. Or, in some cases, with "man's best friend."

Born to be Wild

Published in 1903, *The Call of the Wild* tells the story of Buck, a pampered Saint Bernard/collie mix that is kidnapped from his home in Northern California and sold as a sled dog in the Yukon. His new life forces him to toughen up to the point that he eventually sheds his cloak of domestication altogether and becomes the alpha male of a wolf pack. The book was written by Jack London and is often thought of as his masterpiece.

Better Stock up on Tissue

In *Old Yeller*, Fred Gipson has taken the "a boy and his dog" type of story and given it a heart-wrenching twist. Fourteen-year-old Travis Coates is left in charge of his family when his father goes on a cattle drive. Old Yeller, a yellow, ragged-looking stray dog wanders onto the property in search of food, and Travis' little brother Arliss takes a liking to him. Initially, Travis intensely dislikes the dog, but he learns to respect and eventually love the courageous animal. Sounds like a happy ending in the making, right? Well, you'll have to read the book to find out, but I'd keep the tissue box handy, if I were you. The book was published in 1956 and was turned into a movie in 1957.

Looking for Love

Richard Adams' novel *The Plague Dogs*, published in 1977, tells the grim story of Rowf and Snitter, two dogs that escape from a lab, where they had been subjects of animal experiments. Rowf, born in the lab, is enormously distrustful of humans, but Snitter, once a beloved pet, is determined to find himself and

Rowf a home. As they struggle to survive in the wild, the dogs are pursued by people who want to destroy them, out of fear that they might be infected with the plague.

Taming the Beast

When he wrote *White Fang*, which was published in 1906, Jack London intended it to be a companion novel to his book *The Call of the Wild*. In a complete reversal of the theme of the earlier story, *White Fang* tells the story of a wolf/dog hybrid that grows up wild but eventually becomes civilized. Taken from the wild as a pup, White Fang grows up fierce, because the other dogs in his camp ostracize him. Eventually, he is traded to a scurrilous man, who puts him to work in the dog-fighting ring. Just when things are looking bleak for the protagonist pooch, in walks a hunter named Weedon Scott, who rescues White Fang (in more ways than one).

If you can look at a dog and not feel vicarious excitement and affection, you must be a cat.

–Author Unknown

CONTEMPORARY CANINE TALES

Dog stories are not just limited to the books that you, and your parents before you, read in school. They are very much a part of the modern fiction scene.

So Much for "Man's Best Friend"

Written by Steven King, *Cujo* tells the gruesome story of a Saint Bernard that is bitten by a bat while out hunting and becomes rabid. The dog terrorizes the town of Castle Rock, Maine, killing a number of its residents, including his owner. The majority of the action revolves around a three-day standoff between Cujo and Donna, who, with her four-year-old son, is trapped by the rabid dog in a broken-down car. No spoilers here, but let's just say the story doesn't exactly have a fairytale ending. The book was turned into a gory movie in 1983.

Talk to Me

In *The Dogs of Babel*, published in 2003, Carolyn Parkhurst has invented what must be one of the most creative premises for a book in a long time. Linguistics professor Paul Iverson loses his wife when she falls from a tree and dies. The only witness to her death is Lorelei, the Iverson's Rhodesian ridgeback. Paul's relationship with his wife was a rocky one, and he is haunted by the thought that her death may have been suicide, rather than an accident. How does he get to the truth? He decides to teach Lorelei to talk.

Thou Art a Gossip-mongering Knave!

William Shakespeare may have been a gifted poet and playwright, but, as a husband, the Bard left much to be desired. Much of his home life is shrouded in mystery. Why did he spend most of his married life in London, instead of Stratford? Why did he leave Anne Hathaway nothing but his "second-best bed" in his will? Did husband and wife even like each other? Most Shakespeare aficionados would love to have been a fly on the wall in the Shakespeare house, if only to see how the couple got along. Well, Mr. Hooker (not a fly but a dog) had a ringside seat, and he tells all in *Shakespeare's Dog*, a witty novel by Leon Rooke. Set around the time when Shakespeare is packing up to move to London, the book explores the relationship between the famous poet and his main squeeze as understood by the family dog.

DID YOU KNOW?

The only Shakespeare play with a dog is *The Two Gentlemen of Verona*. A small dog named Crab has a bit part. The breed of dog was not specified.

Smarter than Your Average Pooch

Travis Cornell is walking though the woods contemplating his miserable life, when a terrified but determined golden retriever bars his way. Every time Travis tries to pass, the dog, shaking with fear, stops him. The dog's anxiety is contagious, and soon Travis is convinced that something evil is lurking unseen in the woods. Man and dog flee to the safety of Travis' truck, unable to shake the sense that they are being pursued. So begins Dean Koontz's suspenseful 1987 tale *Watchers*, the story of Einstein, a super-intelligent dog, and The Other, a violent beast that is bent on destroying the pooch. This excellent novel was adapted into a terrible movie starring Corey Haim.

If you are a host to your guest, be a host to his dog also.

–Russian proverb

DOGS ON STAGE AND SCREEN

From the printed page to the stage and screen, dogs also play a prominent role in many of our favorite plays, TV shows and movies.

And the Verdict Is...

In Aristophanes' play *Wasps,* written in 422 BC, a dog named Labes is put on trial for stealing cheese. He is facing the death penalty for his crime, and he brings his pups to the trial, so they can whine for him and perhaps sway his case. In writing the play, Aristophanes was mocking the people of Athens for their propensity to bring lawsuits against each other. Perhaps our overly litigious society could use a modern-day Aristophanes...

All the World's a Stage

A Dog's Life tells the story of a dog named Jack, from the time he is adopted as a pup, through to the end of his life. The musical, written by Sean Grennan, with songs created by Leah Okimoto, explores the relationship between dogs and the people who love them. An actor in costume plays the role of Jack. The play premiered in Kansas City, Missouri, on March 2, 2007.

> *Do not step on the dog's tail, and he will not bite you.*
> –Cameroon proverb

DOGS ON THE TUBE

Dogs have been in plenty of TV programs, sometimes with top billing, other times in smaller roles, but no matter the size of the role, they always steal the show.

Cartoon Canines

☛ Brian, *Family Guy*—Probably the most intelligent, and definitely the most refined, member of the Griffin clan, Brian spends his time reading, drinking cocktails and offering much needed advice to his witless owner, Peter.

☛ Dogbert, *Dilbert*—Not quite your usual loyal-to-a-fault type of dog, Dogbert is a scheming megalomaniac, who gets his kicks by scamming hapless humans, including the management of his owner's workplace.

☛ Droopy, *Droopy*—Although you would never guess it from his appearance, Droopy was actually a shrewd little Basset hound. Most of the characters that shared his animated series underestimated him because the bashful pooch spoke in a dull monotone and had the energy of a sponge. He was created by Tex Avery for MGM, and for reasons that I can't explain, his way of moving and speaking reminds me very much of Alfred Hitchcock from the 1985 series *Alfred Hitchcock Presents*. Droopy graced TV screens throughout North America from 1943 until 1958.

☛ Goofy—An anthropomorphic dog of indeterminate breed, Goofy is a clumsy, rather dimwitted, but ultimately lovable friend to Mickey Mouse. He eventually starred in his own show, *Goof Troop*, in the 1990s.

☛ Gromit, *Wallace and Gromit*—The canine half of the popular British duo, Gromit is a claymation beagle, who lives with his somewhat clueless inventor owner, Wallace.

Although he gives the impression that he is the sensible one of the two, the lovable pooch always happily goes along with whatever crazy schemes Wallace cooks up.

☛ Huckleberry Hound, *The Huckleberry Hound Show*— Created by Hanna-Barbera, the big blue dog with the southern drawl has a good heart but is a little lacking in the intelligence department. Although Huckleberry has fallen largely out of the public eye, in the 1950s, he was one of the most popular cartoon characters on TV.

☛ Pluto—Best known as Mickey Mouse's dog, the yellow bloodhound was a prominent character in many Mickey Mouse cartoons, including the *Mickey Mouse Works* TV series. He went on to star in a number of short cartoons of his own.

☛ Ren, *Ren and Stimpy*—He may not be immediately recognizable as a dog, but Ren is a Chihuahua whose personality is just as unattractive as his physical appearance. In the cartoon, he spent much of his time abusing his sidekick, Stimpy (a cat), and in a few episodes even planned inventive ways to kill him.

☛ Snowy, *The Adventures of Tintin*—A white fox terrier, Snowy bravely accompanies his owner Tintin, a Belgian reporter, wherever Tintin's leads take him and often helps the man out of some dicey situations.

☛ Santa's Little Helper, *The Simpsons*— Santa's Little Helper was a former racing dog adopted into the Simpson's household when he lost one too many races and was sent packing by his previous owner.

☛ Scooby-Doo, *Scooby Doo*—Famous for his huge appreciation of food, the cowardly Great Dane is a reluctant investigator of mysteries that at first seem to be paranormal but are usually discovered to be the work of imaginative criminals with theatrical ability.

- Scrappy, *Scooby Doo*—A Great Dane puppy, Scrappy-Doo is Scooby-Doo's young nephew. A somewhat annoying little go-getter, Scrappy usually charged recklessly into situations that had Scooby running for cover.

- Wile E. Coyote—A member of the large Looney Tunes family, Wile E. Coyote graced the small screen in the *Looney Tunes* and *Merry Melodies* cartoons. He spent most of his time thinking up inventive but hopeless ways of catching the smart-alecky Road Runner and usually only wound up hurting himself.

Canine Characters

- Diefenbaker, *Due South*—Trusty sidekick to Constable Benton Frasier, the lip-reading wolf/dog mix lost his hearing when he pulled Frasier out of a frigid river in the Northwest Territories.

- Eddie, *Frasier*—A feisty Jack Russell terrier, Eddie was a faithful companion to Martin Crane and was foisted upon the reluctant Frasier Crane when he invited Martin to move in with him.

- Lassie—Undoubtedly one of the world's most famous fictional dogs, Lassie was originally a character in a short story. The courageous collie moved to the small screen in the 1950s and has reappeared in many TV series since. The character has also starred in more than 10 live-action movies and in countless full-length books.

- Littlest Hobo—A character in a TV series of the same name, this stray German shepherd wandered from town to town, offering a helping paw to people in need.

- Maximillian, *The Bionic Woman*—Usually called Max, this German shepherd was fitted with a bionic jaw and legs and was adopted by Jamie Sommers, a.k.a. The Bionic Woman, when the lab responsible for creating him wanted to put him down.

☛ Petey, *Our Gang*—Easily recognizable by the black ring around his eye (which was drawn on, by the way), the white pit bull was the canine member of "The Little Rascals."

☛ Wishbone, *Wishbone*—Known as "the little dog with the big imagination," Wishbone was a Jack Russell terrier that daydreamed his way into works of classical fiction.

DID YOU KNOW?

In the hit series *Magnum P.I.*, the character Higgins owned two well-trained Doberman guard dogs named Zeus and Apollo. The dogs hated Magnum, much to Higgin's poorly concealed delight, and often charged or chased him when they saw him.

There is no psychiatrist in the world like a puppy licking your face.

–Bernard Williams

REEL DOGS

I think it is safe to say that there is no movie out there that could not be improved with the addition of a dog. Fortunately, many movies that feature our favorite four-legged friends already exist.

Disney Dogs

101 Dalmatians (1961)—An animated classic, in which 15 Dalmatian puppies (plus 86 other Dalmatians) must be kept out of the clutches of the aptly named Cruella De Vil, who wants to use their coats to make dog-fur jackets. A live-action version of the film, starring Glenn Close as the evil diva, was released in 1996.

Air Bud (1997)—A boy-meets-stray-dog, boy-adopts-stray-dog, stray-dog-changes-boy's-life story, starring a basketball-playing golden retriever named Buddy. The success of this movie spawned a number of direct-to-video sequels, each of which has Buddy learning to play a new sport.

Eight Below (2006)—Based on a true story, this film follows the plight of eight sled dogs left behind at a research base in Antarctica when their owner is forced to evacuate during a powerful storm.

The Fox and the Hound (1981)—One of Disney's less cheerful movies, this animated film tells the tale of a doomed friendship between an orphaned red fox and a bloodhound.

Frankenweenie (1984)—Only 29 minutes long, this canine parody of the classic Frankenstein tale has school-aged Victor Frankenstein putting his science-class knowledge to use to bring his bull terrier, Sparky, back to life after the dog was struck and killed by a car.

The Incredible Journey (1963)—Not to be confused with *Homeward Bound*, the 1993 remake, this classic tells the story of three pets (a Labrador retriever, a bull terrier and a Siamese cat) who are left in the care of a family friend but leave his house and battle the dangers of the Canadian wilderness, as they make their way back home in search of their owners.

Iron Will (1994)—After the death of his father, Will Stoneman must find a way to support himself and his mother, so the teenager takes his father's prized sled dogs and joins an Iditarod-like race that stretches from Winnipeg, Manitoba, to St. Paul, Minnesota.

Lady and the Tramp (1955)—In this animated classic, Lady the pampered cocker spaniel suffers a dip in status when her owners have a new baby, so she leaves her sheltered home and falls in love with a roguish stray named Tramp.

My Dog the Thief (1969)— In this made-for-TV movie, traffic reporter Jack Crandall befriends a stray Saint Bernard after the dog jumps into the back of his helicopter, but little does Jack know that the dog has sticky paws and a taste for priceless jewelry.

The Shaggy Dog (1959)— In Disney's first live-action comedy, Wilby Daniels turns into a sheep dog after he reads the inscription on an ancient, magical ring. The only way he can break the spell and return full-time to his usual teenaged form is to perform an act of virtue.

Snow Dogs (2002)—When his mother passes away, Cuba Gooding Jr.'s character travels from Florida to her home in Alaska and, learning that he has inherited her sled dogs, decides to race them in a local dog-sled competition.

Fido on Film

All Dogs go to Heaven (1989)—In this animated film, a casino-owning dog, murdered by his rival, leaves heaven to return to earth and exact his revenge, befriending a young orphan girl on the way.

Beethoven (1992)—A family movie that pits an uptight father, played by Charles Grodin, against a troublemaking, ill-mannered Saint Bernard that is being targeted by an unscrupulous veterinarian, who wants to use the giant pooch in animal experimentation.

Benji (1974)— In the first of many films starring this character, Benji the stray mutt befriends two young children and then has to find and save them when they are kidnapped.

Cats and Dogs (2001)—Humankind's two favorite pet species are engaged in a covert battle, in which the dogs must foil the nefarious plans of the evil Mr. Tinkles and his feline accomplices, who are trying steal a dog-hair-allergy remedy and change it into a dog-hair-allergy provoker, to turn people against all of dog-kind.

Far From Home: The Adventures of Yellow Dog (1995)—A boy and his Labrador retriever fight for survival after their boat capsizes, separating them from the boy's father and stranding them in the wilds of British Columbia.

Fluke (1995)—Not exactly the feel-good movie of the year, this film tells the story of a man killed in a car accident. Reincarnated as a dog, he becomes the pet of the family he left behind, only to realize that his wife and son might actually be better off without him.

It's a Dog's Life (1955)—A canine rags-to-riches story, this film follows the adventures of a stray bull terrier that is pulled from the dog-fighting ring to become a pedigreed show dog.

My Dog Skip (2000)—Set in the 1940s, this film stars a young Frankie Muniz as Willie, a lonely, socially challenged boy who befriends a troublemaking Jack Russell terrier.

Shiloh (1996)—A touching coming-of-age story about a boy who finds an abused beagle and goes to great lengths to keep him, learning a few lessons about standing up for what you believe in along the way. I have to admit, it brought a tear to my eye...

Turner and Hooch (1989)—A comedy in which a somewhat anal-retentive police detective, played by Tom Hanks, takes in an unkempt (but oh-so-lovable) mastiff named Hooch that is the sole witness to his owner's murder.

Milo and Otis (1986)—a Westernized version of the Japanese live-action film *Koneko Monogatari,* this film tells the story of Otis, a pug, and Milo, an orange tabby, that meet as puppy and kitten and become best friends. The two become separated when Milo is washed downstream, and adventure follows as they try to find each other again.

Best in Show (2000)—This mockumentary, starring Eugene Levy, Catherine O'Hara and Parker Posey, satirizes the world of show dogs and their obsessive owners.

MISCELLANEOUS MUTT STORIES

Not all dogs are recognized for impressive feats or heroic acts. Some pooches are so charismatic, they make the news by just being themselves.

Just a Drink for Me, Please

So a coyote walks into a Chicago sub shop… No, it is not the opening line of a bad joke. It describes the scene in the Loop, the historical centre of downtown Chicago, in April 2007. A Quiznos employee had propped the front door of the shop open, and in strolled the coyote. The animal wandered over to the counter, hoisted himself into the cooler containing the bottled drinks and nestled down amid the glass bottles for a refreshing little snooze. The coyote, dubbed "Adrien" for the animal control officer who trapped him, cooled his heels for about 40 minutes before he was taken away. After being checked over at a nearby animal shelter, the coyote was released in northern Illinois.

Ohhhhmmmm

Agility courses? Sure. Bikejoring? Well, okay. Doggie yoga? Hmmmm…not sure about that one. The medical benefits of yoga have been well documented in humans, so it was just a matter of time before the practice spread to the canine world. Just ask Nanda Dulal, a yogi from Jharkhand, India, who trained his German shepherd, Hritik, to perform a variety of poses, including the sun salutation sequence and cobra. Dulal says he could tell Hritik was interested in learning yoga because the pooch would imitate him as he was doing his daily practice. So Dulal decided to teach his faithful companion a few poses.

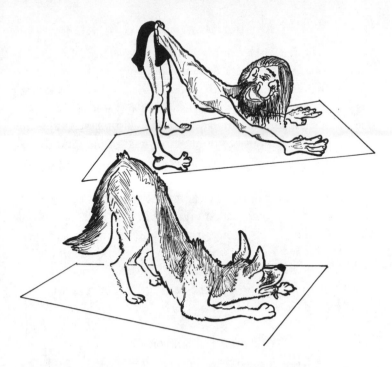

Now, man and dog work through their routines side by side every morning. Dulal swears that the yoga lessons have strengthened his bendy pooch, turning the somewhat feeble pup into an award-winning dog show competitor. Or maybe it's the dog's low-fat diet that has him glowing with health. Like any true yogi, Hritik is a strict vegetarian; he snacks on papayas and cucumbers, instead of the bones and meaty morsels preferred by his canid cousins. I wonder how he feels about that…

DOG FACT The Canaan dog is named for the land God promised to Abraham in the Bible. Canaan is the land's Hebrew name.

Bring on the Doggie Drano

A crew of public works employees from Manakato, Minnesota, had to postpone their work for a few hours when, following the sound of panicked barking, they found Max, a 13-year-old lab, stuck in a 5-inch (38-centimeter) wide culvert under the street. The exhausted dog was only about 50 feet (15 metres) from the nearest entry point, but he could not be coaxed out, and the culvert was far too narrow for any of the work crew to go in after him. So the crew grabbed the long video camera they normally use to inspect drainpipes and put it to a new use—poking Max in the butt. The repeated nudging to his nether regions convinced Max to move forward through the culvert, and eventually he reached an entry point large enough for one of the workers to reach in and pull him out. The shaky pooch was reunited with his owner after the man saw coverage of the rescue by the local media.

The dog is a gentleman;
I hope to go to his heaven, not man's.

–Mark Twain

HEROIC HOUNDS

Dogs have earned our love and respect for good reason.
They are selfless in their devotion and are even willing to
put themselves at risk to protect the ones they love.

Child's Best Friend

Much has been said about the body molds found in the volcano-destroyed town of Pompeii, Rome. Early archaeologists excavating the site realized that the volcanic ash that buried the town buried Pompeii's residents, as well; over time, the bodies decomposed, leaving behind molds. Some of these body casts, including one of a dog that was chained up outside its owners' home, are on display in still-intact buildings on the archaeological site. The chained dog was not the only one in evidence at Pompeii, however. Excavators uncovered evidence of a dog that died while sprawled across a child, apparently trying to shield its young owner from the burning ash. Now, that's what I call devotion!

Heimlich Hound

You often hear stories about dogs that save their owners' lives. Usually the rescue takes the form of the furry, four-legged hero chasing off a potential attacker or waking its owners from a

peaceful slumber because the house is in flames. But this story easily tops them. Toby, a two-year-old golden lab, went beyond the call of duty when he performed a somewhat modified version of the Heimlich maneuver on his choking owner. Debbie Parkhurst, from Cecil County, Maryland, was snacking on an apple when a chunk lodged in her throat. She tried giving herself the Heimlich maneuver using the back of a chair, and when that didn't work, she started pounding on her chest—to no avail. Responding to his owner's distress, Toby stood on his hind legs, put his front paws on her shoulders and pushed her to the floor. Once she was supine, he climbed onto her chest and started jumping up and down. The rough treatment dislodged the apple, and Debbie could breathe freely once more.

DOG FACT

Perhaps it was meant as an ironic statement of loyalty, but in many renditions of the Last Supper, Judas Iscariot is shown with a dog lying at his feet.

Not on My Watch!

The Southwest Wildlife Rehabilitation and Educational Foundation in Scottsdale, Arizona, sees its share of visitors, some welcome, some not so much. The sanctuary is located in the desert, and rattlesnakes have a tendency to slither onto the grounds looking for prey. Pepper, an Australian shepherd mix, is the sanctuary's furry, four-legged rattler detector. When Pepper comes across a snake, he alerts staff members with shrill barks and circles the offending reptile until it can be scooped into a bucket and released into the desert. However, in August 2006, Pepper had to change his tactics a little. A determined snake was going for Pepper's special friend, a 14-year-old coyote named Kachina, and Pepper had to place himself between the snake and the coyote's pen to keep the reptile at bay until human backup could arrive. By the time the snake was safely removed from the scene, Pepper had been bitten on the leg.

He was rushed to the Sonora Veterinary Hospital in Phoenix, where he was treated with antivenin. Twice. The tough little mutt bounced back quickly from his nasty experience and was soon back at work, patrolling the grounds. When he is not snake detecting, Pepper can often be found sleeping back to back with Kachina, the two animals separated only by the chain-link fence of the coyote's pen.

Just Call Me Twiggy

"Skinny" isn't normally a sought-after characteristic in a police dog, but it certainly helped Indy, a member of the K-9 force in Edmonton, Alberta, perform his public service duties. On January 13, 2007, a woman was ripped out of what must have been a very deep sleep when a strange man crawled into her bed. She managed to call the police before the man grabbed a hammer and attacked her. When officers arrived on the scene, they could see her inside the house, struggling with her assailant, but they could not get in to help her, because the man had barricaded the door. One of the officers was able to force the door open slightly, and Indy squeezed through the narrow gap. The dog took down the attacker and held him until the more portly, two-legged officers were able to make their way inside.

Even the tiniest poodle is lionhearted, ready to do anything to defend home, master and mistress.

–Louis Sabin

DOGS BEHAVING BADLY

Well, we can't be on our best behavior all the time.
Even dogs have their off days.

All Shook Up

You've heard of a kid in candy shop. And a bull in a china shop. How about a dog in a teddy bear museum? Sounds like a bad combination, doesn't it? Well, the insurance company in charge of a collection of priceless teddy bears didn't think so. Wookey Hole Caves museum in Somerset, England, was planning a teddy bear exhibit, and the insurance company would only allow the bears to be displayed if a security dog was hired to keep them safe. So, along came Barney, a four-year-old Doberman pinscher. Perhaps someone should have made it clear to him that he was meant to be protecting the bears.

The first victim was Mabel, a Steiff bear manufactured in Germany in 1909 and, at one time, the beloved toy of Elvis Presley. Mabel had recently sold at auction for £40,000, but Barney was not put off by the expensive price tag. He lunged for the unsuspecting bear, partially tearing its head from its body. Barney's handler managed to pry the wounded toy from Barney's jaw, but not without the loss of a great deal of stuffing. Worse, once Barney lost possession of the bear, the dog went mad. He ran amok among the teddy bears, leaving a trail of destruction in his wake, and had to be wrestled to the ground to stop the carnage. By the time he was finished, furry bear bits littered the floor. Stuffing was scattered everywhere, and bears that had not been torn asunder were covered with a slimy coating of Barney's drool.

No one is sure just what made Barney lose his cool, but his handler suggests that Mabel may have had a "rogue" scent that set the dog off. (Fried peanut butter and banana sandwiches, perhaps? Just a thought.) In all, Barney's little rampage caused more than £60,000 worth of damage to the bears. Mabel's owner sent for what was left of his bear, but it is likely that, like Humpty Dumpty, it could not be put back together again. As for Barney, the disgraced pooch was sent to live out the remainder of his days on a farm.

Do You Smell Something on my Suitcase?

As part of their battle to stop the flow of illegal drugs through their country, Thai law enforcement agents use sniffer dogs at airports to search passengers and their baggage. In a shining example of killing two flies with one blow (so to speak), King Bhumibol Adulyadej set up a program that took strays off the streets and trained them to become police dogs. Mok and Lai were two such dogs. The mixed-breed mutts were pressed into service at the Chiang Rai Airport, near the so-called "Golden Triangle," a well-known opium producing area. The canine team held two of the highest seizure records in the country, but that wasn't enough to save their jobs. In June 2007, the two furry officers, which should have been the pride of Thailand's narcotics team, were relieved of their duties under a cloud of shame. It seems that Mok and Lai had suffered a lapse in manners, peeing on traveler's baggage, and "rubbing up" against female passengers in a most inappropriate manner. The canine agents were accused of "unbecoming conduct" and were banished to a nearby farm. They now spend their days mingling with pigs and chickens, which presumably are not bothered by the dogs' lack of broughtupsy.

You Call that Security?

Security personnel in the FLZ factory in Bor, Yugoslavia, were stumped. Somehow, a crafty crook was slipping past their defenses and making off with hundreds of dollars worth of copper wire every night. Security staff could find no signs of forced entry, and Džeki, the guard dog, never detected the thief's presence. Finally, the company decided to install closed-circuit TV cameras. The recorded footage revealed, much to everyone's surprise, that the burglaries were an inside job. While the security guards were outside patrolling the grounds, Džeki was sneaking into the storeroom and helping herself to the copper, which she then buried in the yard. Apparently, the copper wire was coated, and Džeki liked the smell of it. By the time she was caught, the sneaky pooch had pilfered thousands of dollars worth of wiring. The company was able to recover most of the stolen goods by sweeping the grounds with a metal detector, but at least $300 worth has still not been located. As for Džeki, she was allowed to keep her job, but I'm guessing her human coworkers keep a close eye on her if she goes anywhere near the storeroom.

Do You Smell Gas?

The Dodson family from Norman, Oklahoma, got the surprise of their lives when they returned home one day to find piles of rubble strewn across the lot where their house should have been standing. Where, in fact, it had been standing only a few hours earlier, when they left it. Sitting filthy and trembling, but basically unhurt, amid the wreckage was Jake, the Dodson's three-month-old Rottweiler. Fire investigators think the curious pup must have been playing with gas line switch and accidentally turned it on. The house filled with natural gas, which was ignited by a spark from the water heater when it clicked on. The result? An explosion strong enough to blow the roof almost six inches (16 centimeters) off the frame before reducing the rest of the structure to a mass of twisted timber and broken bricks. I know of one little puppy that won't be left unsupervised in the future…

No Need for Candles

Peggy, a six-month-old Rottweiler cross, discovered firsthand just how hazardous to one's health a sweet tooth can be. The young pooch was trying to reach a chocolate birthday cake that was sitting on the stovetop of her East Sleekburn, Northumberland, home, when she accidentally turned on one of the burners. The kitchen was soon engulfed in flames. Peggy retreated to the bathroom and climbed into the tub, where she survived by breathing relatively smoke-free air through the drain hole. By the time firefighters dragged her from the burning building, her grip on life was tenuous. The tiny troublemaker was fitted with an oxygen mask and underwent 45 minutes of heart massage before she was fully revived. In the end, Peggy made it through her ordeal with no permanent damage. The same cannot be said for the kitchen. Or the birthday cake.

A Happy Ending All Around

Things were not going well for poor little Pepper, a red-eared slider turtle. Shelby Terihay, from Brandon, Florida, had moved her pet turtles indoors to a temporary home in the bathtub, hoping to protect them from the cool temperatures outside. She did not realize that the turtles faced an equally dangerous threat inside the house—Bella, the golden retriever. The dog wandered into the bathroom, saw the unsuspecting turtles lounging in the tub and swallowed Pepper. When Shelby returned to the bathroom a few minutes later to check on her aquatic pets, she realized she was one short. After an emergency call to the vet, Shelby and her parents made Bella vomit, and, along with the dog's stomach contents, out came a still-living (though presumably shaken) Pepper. The turtle's shell was shattered, but otherwise the little trooper was in good health, despite having spent about 10 minutes in Bella's stomach and suffering various indignities on its journey from bathtub to belly. Bella should also be grateful that the turtle was rescued. According to the vet, having a turtle in her tummy would have eventually killed Bella, as well.

AMAZING FEATS

Dogs are known for being clever, tough and resourceful—but some pooches really outshine their furry peers.

A Real Cliff Hanger-on Cliffhanger

Margie Brett was vacationing in Ilfracombe, Devon, enjoying a ramble along the cliff with her Staffordshire bull terrier, Bush, when the dog ran off in pursuit of a deer and vanished. When no amount of searching revealed the dog, Margie returned dogless to her home in Oxfordshire. Two weeks after Bush's disappearance, Margie heard a news report about two climbers stranded on some cliffs in Devon near where she had been walking. The climbers had apparently run into trouble while trying to reach a dog that was stuck on a ledge more than 100 feet (30 meters) above sea level. Margie contacted the coastguard, which passed the call to a nearby Royal Air Force base, and a rescue team was sent out as part of a training exercise. Bush had fallen more than 195 feet (60 meters), before landing on the thin ledge that was her less-than-comfy home for two weeks. Although she managed to stave off dehydration by drinking from a waterfall, and her rescuers found a pile of crow feathers next to her on the ledge, Bush was in pretty bad shape. After a few weeks' recovery in a nearby animal hospital, she was reunited with her happy family, none the worse for wear, though perhaps a little wiser.

You Want the Doggie Hospital, Two Doors Down

Doctors and nurses working in hospitals throughout Los Angeles, California, probably see more than their share of strange sights from day to day. In fact, many might have even become blasé about it. But I'm thinking that even the most seasoned of them must have been taken aback when they saw Buddy, a six-year-old German shepherd mix, patiently waiting

his turn in the waiting room of the Kaiser Permanente Hospital in Bellflower. On October 4, 2006, Buddy was struck by a car and suffered a dislocated leg. He limped to the hospital's emergency room, stood in front of the automatic doors until they opened, then went into the waiting room and lay down. Security was called, and the dog was forced back outside—but only temporarily. Buddy limped back inside and, this time, refused to budge. Emergency room staff called animal control, which collected the injured pooch. He was taken to a nearby animal shelter, where people who are trained to heal dogs patched up his wounds. With the help of the microchip in his neck, the shelter staff tracked down Buddy's owners, and he was returned home to resume his duties as guard dog for an equipment yard.

WHAT WERE THEY THINKING?

Let me share with you a universal truth. For every story you read about a dog that acts strangely, you will find a dozen more about people whose behavior is even more unfathomable. And that's a conservative estimate...

Wanted: Dog Bodyguards

"Desperate times call for desperate measures," as the saying goes. The Malaysian crime syndicate must have been desperate, indeed, when they took out a contract for almost US$30,000 on the heads of two dogs. Lucky and Flo, two black labs working with the Malaysian police force, are sniffer dogs, trained not to search for narcotics but to seek out polycarbonate, a chemical used in the manufacture of DVDs. The two dogs—the only ones in the world trained to detect pirated DVDs—are part of a joint effort between the Motion Picture Society of America (MPAA) and Malaysian law enforcement to sniff out those involved in a DVD piracy ring. The MPAA sent Lucky and Flo to Asia to help break up the ring and stop the film industry's hemorrhaging of money (an estimated $6.1 billion annually). The pooches have taken a huge bite out of the piracy ring's profits—in one month alone, they sniffed out more than $3.5 million worth of contraband DVDs, including pirated films and child pornography, which were confiscated by police. So, you can understand why the Malaysian crime syndicate would want the dogs out of the way. To keep the hardworking pooches safe, extra security measures have been implemented, and the dogs are constantly moved around.

Every Vote Counts

Duncan M. McDonald, an Australian shepherd-terrier mix, is clearly not performing his civic duty. The lazy pooch was stricken from the King County, Washington, voter rolls after having been sent absentee ballots for three elections. Apparently, the dog's owner, Jane Balogh, registered him as a voter "to make a point that anyone could vote, even an animal." She listed the phone in Duncan's name, then used the phone bill as identification when mailing in the voter registration form. When the first election came around, Balogh scrawled "VOID" across the ballot and even added a paw print as a signature. Balogh was charged with making a false statement to a public official. As for Duncan, he's waiting for the day when a credit card in his name appears in the mail.

Muzzle that Dog Owner!

I'm betting the police didn't see this one coming. On April 4, 2007, two officers were walking down the street in Cova da Moura, Portugal, when they spotted a man walking a pit bull terrier, the dog wearing neither a harness nor a muzzle. According to Portugal's dangerous dog legislation, enacted in 2004, all breeds classified as dangerous must be muzzled in public and be kept on a lead no more than 3 feet (1 meter) long. When the police officers approached the man, the man became combative and turned the dog loose, ordering it to attack the officers. Proving that not all pit bulls are naturally aggressive, the dog beat a hasty retreat. The man then turned on the officers himself, biting one on the wrist and breaking the other's finger. Both officers were treated in hospital and released. The dog owner, meanwhile, was placed under house arrest, while the police tried to track down his missing mutt. I wonder if the man will have to wear a muzzle when he's finally allowed to leave the house…

A Baaad Scam

Okay, let's walk through this together. Which of the following characteristics would you expect your poodle puppy to have? Soft fur? Yep. Gentle eyes? Sure. A short tail? Maybe. Hooves? Now, just a minute… As unbelievable as it might seem, thousands of rich Japanese consumers were tricked into believing that they were buying a miniature poodle, when in fact the animal they took home with them was actually a lamb. Miniature poodles are the latest must-have pet in Japan, and they regularly sell for more than US$2400. An unscrupulous (though admirably bold) Internet company imported lambs from the UK and Australia and passed them off on unsuspecting buyers as pedigreed poodles. Apparently, sheep are rare in Japan, so most people have no idea what a lamb looks like. And, at a bargain price of US$1200, wannabe poodle owners quickly snapped up the furry imposters. However, the scam began to unfold when movie star Maiko Kawakami showed a picture of her "poodle" on a talk show, telling the host that her new pet refused to eat dog food and never barked. She was reportedly crushed to learn that the dog was actually a lamb. Soon, hundreds of people were contacting police and filing complaints that they had been similarly conned. I don't know…you'd think the hooves would have been a tip-off.

Toothless Accusation

Britain's Dangerous Dogs Act of 1991 was enacted to keep the public safe from, and to control the ownership of, dog breeds that lawmakers labeled aggressive by nature. Under this legislation, any dog that shows aggression can be confiscated and destroyed. The offending dog is tried in court and, if found guilty of aggression, is usually put to sleep. Thirteen-year-old Beth was facing such a fate in a court in Aberporth, Wales, for allegedly growling at two elderly women. According to the prosecution, the women were "left distressed" by the dog's actions, and the prosecutor was recommending Beth be put down as a threat to public safety. But the defense had a trick up its sleeve. The lawyer defending Beth called the aged pooch to the witness stand and opened her jaws. There was not one single tooth to be found in her mouth. The lawyer pointed out the lack of dentition and asked the court how they could even consider classifying a dog with no teeth as dangerous. According to Beth's owner, Maxine Turner, the dog's teeth had fallen out more than two years earlier. "She can't even chew her dog food because she hasn't got a tooth in her head," Maxine told the court. "What is she going to do—lick people to death?" The court found in Beth's favor, and the toothless pooch was allowed to return home to live another day.

Always Read the Signs

Strong powers of observation are not among the attributes of the three burglars who broke into an abandoned nursing home in Gainesville, Georgia. The trio entered the building to pilfer its copper pipes and wiring. What they must have overlooked were the signs outside that read, "Caution! Gainesville Police Department K-9 training facility—Keep Out." As the crooks went about their business, police K-9 handlers and their four-legged charges strolled into the building, catching the thieves in the act. The thieves dropped their tools and fled. Now, let's see. Three panicked crooks on the run. An entire unit of highly trained police dogs. You see where I'm going with this? Let's just say that things did not turn out as the criminals hoped. One of the trio surrendered without incident, another was taken down by a well-placed bite to the butt and the last was quickly tracked to a nearby store, where he was found cowering behind a trash bin. Perhaps the crooks should have spent less time thieving and more time reading.

Driving Mrs. Li

I would love to have seen the police officers' reactions when they arrived at the scene of a traffic accident in Hohhot, Mongolia, to find a somewhat shaky pooch behind the wheel. When asked to explain the circumstances of the accident, Mrs. Li, owner of the dog (and the car), calmly explained to the attending officers that while she was teaching her dog to drive, he swerved into oncoming traffic. And why was she teaching her dog to drive, you ask. Well, apparently the curious pooch always kept a close eye on Mrs. Li as she was driving and enjoyed draping his paws over the steering wheel, so she decided it was only fair to let the pooch "have a try." While Mrs. Li worked the accelerator and the brakes, her dog took the wheel. Why not the other way around? Well, that would just be silly.

WHO'S AFRAID OF THE BIG, BAD WEREWOLF?

No account of canine folklore would be complete without a tip of the hat to everyone's favorite furry villain, the werewolf.

From Whence They Came

Many theories offer explanations for the origins of the belief in werewolves. One of the most interesting and sensible theories I've heard suggests that it arose in prehistoric times, when early hunters draped themselves in pelts of the animals they had killed, in the belief that some of the animals' qualities would pass to the one wearing the skin. This idea is prevalent in cultures around the world, which might explain why werewolves, or werewolf-like creatures, appear in the folklore of many countries.

Medieval Menaces

During the Medieval Inquisition in Europe, fanatics were not only hunting down and burning supposed witches, they were also keeping their little judgmental eyes open for werewolves. In those days, people believed that, to become a werewolf, you made a pact with the devil. So, if someone was accused of heresy, he had to watch his back, especially if there were reports in the neighborhood of livestock being killed during the night. And really, with the amount of forest and wildlife in Europe during medieval times, what community didn't lose a few chickens or sheep to predators?

I Wanna be a Star

It is pretty safe to say that the modern incarnation of the werewolf has little in common with the beast as he was known in the past. We can thank Hollywood and, to a lesser extent, popular fiction for the werewolf as we know him today. For example, traditionally, one could not become a werewolf unwillingly. The idea of a victim being afflicted with lycanthrope after being bitten or scratched by another werewolf seems to be a relatively recent invention. Originally, anyone who so desired could become a werewolf simply by making a pact with the devil (though how one might have actually gone about making such a pact isn't clear). Also, the werewolf as first imagined did not transform from human to canine form only during a full moon; he could switch at will and did so at night to indulge his base urges. Another Hollywoodism is the belief that werewolves can only be killed with a silver bullet. No such belief exists in traditional werewolf lore.

A Werewolf by Any Other Name…

Werewolves have held a prominent role in the folklore of many countries throughout Europe. What follows is a sampling of words for werewolf from different European nations.

Andorra—*home llop*

Bulgaria—*valkolak*

Denmark, Sweden, Norway—*varulv*

Estonia—*libahunt*

Finland—*ihmissusi*

France—*loup-garou*

Hungary—*farkasember*

Iceland—*kveld-ulf*

Ireland—*faoladh* or *conriocht*

Lithuania—*vilkolakis*

Macedonia—*vrkolak*

The Netherlands—*weerwolf*

Poland—*wilkołak*

Portugal—*lobisomem*

Russia—*vourdalak*

Spain—*hombre lobo*

Turkey—*kurtadam*

DID YOU KNOW?

The word lycanthrope is Greek in origin, a combination of *lykos*, meaning "wolf," and *anthropos*, meaning "man." It comes to us from Greek mythology. Lycaon, king of Arcadia, received an unexpected visit from Zeus, who had disguised himself as a traveler. Lycaon recognized the god despite his disguise and tried to kill him by slipping human flesh into his food. Zeus realized what Lycaon was up to, and, with a comment about matching the king's outer appearance to his inner self, turned him into a wolf.

Bad to the Bone

Romanian folklore speaks of werewolf-like creatures known as *pricolici*. These nasty beasties take the form of abnormally large dogs or wolves and are believed to be souls that have shunned "the light," preferring instead to prowl the Earth, inflicting pain and misery on unsuspecting people. Men who were especially violent or vicious in life were thought to return after death as pricolici.

Belief in these paranormal pooches lingers in the Romanian countryside to this day. People occasionally report encounters with huge, unusually fierce wolves or dogs, which they claim appear from nowhere, move without a sound and attack with a level of viciousness that is unprecedented in your average, non-paranormal canine.

Loup-ga-who?

In Louisiana, naughty children no doubt lay trembling in their beds at night, straining to hear the footfalls of the dreaded *rougarou*. According to Louisiana legend, the creature has the body of a man and the head of a wolf or dog. It prowls at night, snacking on misbehavers, including lapsed Catholics and children who do not heed their parents. As with most werewolf legends, during daylight the rougarou returns to its human form. The name rougarou is a variation of the French term loup-garou.

Just Your Friendly, Neighborhood Werewolf

The global werewolf community must hang their heads in
shame when they contemplate their Scottish cousin, the *wulver*.
Born of Shetland Islands' folklore, the wulver is not your typical, bloodthirsty, havoc-wreaking shapeshifter but a rather low-
energy sort of werewolf, preferring to spend his days lazing
around on a rock (known as the Wulver's Stone), catching fish.
The wulver has the body of a man—a rather hirsute man,
apparently, as he is covered with short, dark brown hair—and
the head of a wolf. A peaceful creature, for a werewolf, he keeps
mostly to himself and even has a benevolent streak, sometimes
leaving his catch of the day on the windowsills of the poor.
Now that's my kind of werewolf…

DID YOU  KNOW?

Some historical accounts of lycanthropy might have a rational,
if grim, explanation. There is a school of thought that believes
the carnage attributed to werewolves may have actually been the
work of serial killers. Modern-day serial killers have been known
to mutilate and eat the flesh of their victims, just as werewolves
supposedly did.

MORE PARANORMAL POOCHES

They might not have the status of werewolves, but other creepy canines have earned themselves reputations for causing havoc in countries around the world.

More Annoying than Frightening

As far as nasty canines of folklore go, the *pesanta* is pretty tame. This creature of Spanish folklore is really more of a nuisance than a threat. Described as a massive, black dog with paws of steel, Catalonia's pesanta creeps into people's homes and sits on their chest, restricting their airflow and giving them horrible nightmares. The creature's paws are said to be full of holes to prevent it from stealing, so I guess your good silver is safe, even if your peace of mind is not.

I Prefer the White...

The next time you pass through South or Central America, you might want to keep an eye out for the *cadejo*. The paranormal pooch shows itself during the night to travelers. Just look for an unkempt, cow-sized dog with burning red eyes and cloven feet. It should be easy to spot. If the creepy canine you encounter is white, you're in luck; you've run into the good cadejo—the one that protects travelers. Your journey, at least while the helpful pooch is around, will be problem free. However, if a black cadejo blocks your path, expect the worst. The black cadejo is trouble. It stalks its prey, making just enough noise to let him know he's not alone. Once the victim is completely unnerved, the black cadejo strikes, tearing him to bits. If one of these evil creatures has you in its sights, you'd better hope the dark beast's white counterpart is nearby. Only the white cadejo is mighty enough to beat back an attacking black cadejo.

The Guatemalan cadejo seems to have a soft spot for drunks and is said to protect them from anyone who would do them harm. I wonder if that includes irate spouses…

DID YOU KNOW?

The *tayra*, a type of weasel indigenous to South and Central America, is colloquially known as the cadejo and might be the creature that inspired the legend of the black and white cadejos. Must be one big weasel…

Part Bear, Part Dog, All Trouble

According to the legends of some Native American cultures, a giant wolf-like creature prowls the borderlands between Alaska and the Northwest Territories. Sightings of this fierce canine, known as the *waheela*, were especially common in the Nahanni Valley (also known as Headless Valley, thanks to the nasty pooch) and still trickle in from the area today. The waheela is described as a massive, stocky wolf with a long, snow-white coat. Its back legs are said to be shorter than its front ones, and its huge paws have widely spaced toes. As for its personality, the waheela seems to be antisocial. It shuns the pack life preferred by true wolves and lives alone in remote, largely inhospitable areas, stalking and beheading anyone foolish enough to wander into its territory. Native Americans believed the wolf was an evil spirit, but cryptozoologists that have taken an interest in the waheela suggest that it might be a modern-day version of the prehistoric bear-dog or dire wolf. I like to think it is Bigfoot's faithful companion.

Hairy Harbinger of Death

The black dog of British folklore strikes fear into the heart of anyone who sees it. However, unlike the werewolf, the black dog does not have a reputation as a vicious killer; instead, it foretells death. Whenever the phantom dog shows itself, those unfortunate enough to lay eyes on it will either lose a loved one or die themselves. The black dog is said to be freakishly large, with eyes that glow.

We Do Things Differently Around Here
The people of Meriden, Connecticut, also speak of a black dog that signifies death is on the way. However, they do not subscribe to the massive, scary-looking, black-dog-of-death thing—theirs is the Black Dog of West Peak, a small, sad-looking pup that seems to bask in the company of people. According to local folklore, if you see the little pooch once, you will have good luck; if you see it twice, your luck will turn sour; see it a third time, and someone is going to die.

It's a Grim Job, but Someone's Gotta Do It

Yet another black dog of British folklore is the Church Grim. This particular black dog is not much of a threat, unless you are in the habit of prowling around graveyards, wreaking havoc. The Church Grim is responsible for protecting the souls of those buried in the church's hallowed ground from witches, the devil and anyone else intent on disturbing their eternal rest. However, the supernatural pooch was known to have done more than a little disturbing of its own—it seems the Grim had a penchant for ringing the church bells during the night.

No matter how much you feed a wolf,
he will always return to the forest.

–Russian proverb

DOGGONE SUPERSTITIONS

*Throughout the ages, people have held some pretty
strange beliefs about our four-legged friends.*

☛ Folklore has it that a dog with an intact dewclaw is immune to a snakebite.

☛ If a dog eats grass, it will rain.

☛ If a dog howls three times, someone has died.

☛ A chance encounter with a strange dog, especially a Dalmatian, will bring you good luck, but if a strange dog follows you, it will bring you bad luck.

☛ Seeing a lone fox is lucky, but seeing a few foxes together is unlucky.

☛ Looking a wolf in the eye causes blindness.

☛ If a horse steps onto the pawprint of a wolf, the horse will go lame.

☛ In the Middle Ages, powdered wolf liver was believed to relieve the pain of childbirth.

☛ Dogs that howl on Christmas Eve will go mad by the year's end.

☛ Ancient Greeks believed that dogs could sense evil.

☛ In medieval times, a dog that had bitten someone was killed because it was believed that if the dog later contracted rabies, the bite victim would also contract the disease. The remedy for a bite from a mad dog was to eat part of the dog, such as part of its liver or some of its fur.

☞ In England, it was considered a sign of good luck to see three white dogs together.

☞ Scots believed that if an unfamiliar dog entered your house, you would soon meet a new friend.

☞ In some Native American cultures, a sick person was put to bed with a dog in the belief that the illness would transfer from the afflicted person's body into the body of the dog.

☞ When you see an ambulance, you must pinch your nose or hold your breath until you see a black or brown dog. If you don't, you will have bad luck.

☞ To get rid of a persistent cough, pluck a hair from your head, put it between two slices of buttered bread and feed it to a dog while saying, "Eat well, you hound; may you be sick and I be sound."

☞ If you dream about a dog, you will have trustworthy friends.

☞ Hearing a dog bark first thing in the morning means that you are about to receive bad news and that difficult times are on the way.

DID YOU KNOW?

The belief that dogs can sense death might actually have some science to back it up. Scientists suggest that chemical changes in the body of a dying person cause the person to smell different. Because dogs can detect the change in smell, it's possible that they can tell when a person is sick or dying.

Killing the dog does not heal the bite.

–Chinese proverb

MYTHOLOGICAL MUTTS

Most of us have heard of at least a few mythological characters, such as Hercules and Zeus. But many people don't realize that the mythologies of many ancient civilizations had canine characters, as well.

Hades Hound

Here's a dog that won't win any "Most Attractive Dog of the Year" awards. Cerberus, the guardian of Hades in Greek mythology, is a fierce, three-headed hellhound that is often depicted as having the tail of a serpent. His job is to greet the souls of the newly departed (usually with some good, old-fashioned, terror-instilling) and grant them passage into the Land of the Dead. If any souls try to sneak back out of Hades, Cerberus eats them. He is also responsible for keeping living people out of the Land of the Dead, which he usually accomplishes by tearing them to bits (and thereby, ironically, ensuring their welcome into the Land of the Dead, albeit in a body-free form).

Hercules was one of only a few able to defeat Cerberus. During a fit of temporary insanity instigated by the jealous god Hera, Hercules murdered his own wife and children. As penance for his crime, the Oracle of Delphi told Hercules that he would have to complete 12 seemingly impossible labors, one of which was to defeat Cerberus. Hercules overpowered the hound and dragged him out of Hades, up to the surface world.

DID YOU KNOW?

Wolfsbane is a plant that supposedly originated when Cerberus drooled on some weeds when Hercules brought him up to the surface world. According to medieval lycanthrope lore, were-wolves have an aversion to the plant.

Twice the Fun

Another dog of Greek mythology with more heads than any self-respecting canine should have is Orthrus, brother of Cerberus. This two-headed canine is also often depicted with the tail of a serpent. Although perhaps not as intimidating as his brother, Orthrus is nasty nonetheless. According to myth, Hercules killed Orthrus, while Orthrus was performing his duty as watch-dog to a herd of red-skinned cattle owned by the Titan Geryon. Orthrus is often credited with being the father of the Sphinx.

Forever Faithful

Argos, the faithful furry friend of Ulysses, exemplifies the loy-alty that makes us love our canine companions so deeply. In Homer's epic poem, the *Odyssey*, Ulysses, King of Ithaca, dis-guises himself as a beggar when he returns to his kingdom after having been away for more than 20 years. He wants to see if his wife and friends have remained loyal to him during his long absence, and how his subjects speak of their absent king. As Ulysses wanders unrecognized among his people, he realizes that he has been all but forgotten. Everyone has given him up for dead. Well, almost everyone. Argos, long past his prime, greets his owner with a wag of his tail before allowing himself to finally slip away to wherever it is that Greek legend sends dogs when they die. The pooch, which had been waiting for his owner's return, had clung to life, despite his advanced age and weakness, just to see Ulysses one last time.

The Fox and the Hound

Greek mythology is littered with canines: hellhounds, hunting dogs, faithful companions…you name it. One of the most interesting canine-containing myths is the story of Laelaps and the Teumessian fox. Laelaps, a magical hunting dog who was destined to always catch his prey, passed through a number of hands before he was offered as a gift from King Minos to Procris of Athens. Procris had helped cure Minos of a particularly unpleasant curse (which I will not sully these pages by describing), slapped on him by his wife to keep him from his philandering ways. To show his gratitude, Minos passed Laelaps on to Procris. Procris' husband thought it would be clever to set the dog on the Teumessian fox, another magical canine, which was destined to never be caught. The two raced around for ages, until Zeus, offended by the contradiction in destinies, put an end to the chase by turning both animals to stone.

DID YOU KNOW?

In Roman mythology, the god Mars has two sacred animals; one is the wolf, the other is the woodpecker.

You're a Star

Dogs are so enmeshed in the human consciousness that we even see them represented in the night sky. Canis Major, the Great Dog constellation, has been recognized since at least ancient Greek times, although different civilizations had their own interpretations of which dog the stars represent. The ancient Romans believed the constellation was Europa's guard dog, which failed in its duties when it did not protect her from being kidnapped. In classical Europe, the constellation was often cited as Laelaps or as Cephalus' hound, an animal famous for its speed. In ancient Greece, Canis Major was believed to be one of Orion's hunting dogs, and that is how the constellation is known today, at least in the Western world. Sirius, the Dog Star, is part of Canis Major and is located at the dog's shoulder.

DID YOU KNOW?

In ancient times, Sirius, a blue-white star, was sometimes described as red. Ancient Romans believed that if the star was red, one of their many gods was angry, so they sacrificed red dogs to appease the incensed deity.

No Afterlife for You!

The ancient Egyptians worshiped a huge pantheon, many of which have made it into today's popular culture. One of the most familiar gods is Anubis, guardian of the scales of truth. Depicted with the body of a man and the head of a jackal, Anubis is responsible for preparing the bodies of the dead for the afterlife, removing and washing the internal organs before placing them in canopic jars. His most important task, though, is to weigh the dead person's heart. If the heart is light, Anubis leads the soul to Osiris, who then allows it to pass into the Land of the Dead. However, if the heart is heavy, Anubis feeds the soul to Ammut—a demon with the head of a crocodile, the torso of a lion and the backend of a hippo—denying the person an afterlife.

DID YOU KNOW?

Ancient Egyptians used sweet-smelling herbs to preserve their deceased loved ones because they believed Anubis used his canine sense of smell to judge whether or not a soul was pure enough to enter the Land of the Dead.

He's Got Souls

Although he is not as well known as Anubis, in his day, Wepwawet was held in high esteem by the ancient Egyptians. The god was usually depicted as a wolf or jackal, or as a man with a human body and a wolf or jackal head. He was originally worshiped as a war god, especially in his city, Lycopolis (Greek for "city of wolves"), but he eventually came to be seen as the son of Anubis and was believed to lead the souls of the dead to the underworld.

Which End is Which?

Two-headed dogs were not exclusive to Greek mythology; legends of such a creature also exist in several African countries, including Angola and the Congo. The *kozo*, as it was known,

differs from Orthrus in that, instead of sharing a neck, its two heads were on the opposite sides of its body—one in the usual location and one where the creature's butt should be. Sort of makes you wonder how the poor beast sat down, doesn't it? The kozo was a guardian of the underworld, patrolling the passage into the Land of the Dead, to prevent souls from returning to the land of the living.

Not Exactly a God's Best Friend

In Norse mythology, Fenrir was an enormous, evil wolf who was destined to end the world. To prevent this from happening, the gods caged Fenrir when he was a pup, then eventually chained him to a rock one mile (1.6 kilometres) underground. Because the wolf was too strong to be held by ordinary chain, the gods used a magical binding, made, surprisingly, of ribbon. Although Fenrir was unable to free himself, he was destined to break the ribbon on the day of Ragnarök, the final battle between the gods and the giants. He would side with the giants, seek out Odin—the god of death, war and poetry—and tear him into tiny pieces, effectively bringing about the end of the world.

DID YOU KNOW?

Fenrir had two sons, Hati and Skoll (although how he managed to find a mate is a mystery—after all, he spent most of his life either in a cage or tied to a rock underground, but I digress...). Skoll chased the chariot containing the Sun across the sky, and Hati pursued the Moon.

Don't Look Now

The Wild Hunt is a common theme in many European mythologies. During the hunt, Odin (or other mythological figure) led a group of ghostly hunters across the night sky. Most of the huntsmen were on horseback, and many were accompanied by hounds. It was, in fact, the sound of the baying hounds that signaled the hunt was on—most people could not actually see the hunt in progress. Anyone who did see the Wild Hunt was in danger of being kidnapped and forced to join in the pursuit or brought to the Land of the Dead, never to return. The Wild Hunt was used to explain thunderstorms and was also thought to be an omen of war or a plague. It had a variety of names, including Odin's Hunt, Gabriel's Hounds and my personal favorite, "The Devil's Dandy Dogs."

DID YOU KNOW?

Odin was often depicted with his two wolves, Geri and Freki, usually with one on each side of him.

The End is Near

Garm, another canine of Norse Mythology, was a huge wolf with a perpetually bloodstained chest. He was one of the guardians of Hel, the Norse land of the dead. According to legend, Garm's howling would signal the day of Ragnarök, setting in motion the final battle. During the battle, Garm would kill, and be killed by Tyr, the god who fed Fenrir while he was caged and tied up underground.

Brrrrrrrrr.....

Inuit mythology speaks of an evil spirit named Keelut, an entity from the underworld that takes the shape of a huge, hairless dog prowling the frozen landscape. If Keelut comes across an unwary traveler during his wanderings, he stalks the person, toying with him, before unleashing his rage and tearing his victim to bits. I guess if I was a hairless dog in the Arctic, I'd be a little cranky, too.

From the Dead Come the Living

The Mexican hairless dog, officially known as the Xoloitzcuintle, gets its name from Xolotl, the Aztec god who guarded the Sun as it made its way through the underworld each night. Xolotl, depicted as a skeleton with a dog's head and ragged ears, was associated with sickness, deformity and bad luck. He and his brother Quetzalcoatl went to the Land of Death, gathered the bones they found there and brought them to back to the present world, to create humankind.

DID YOU  **KNOW?**

One of Xolotl's dogs, most likely a Xoloitzcuintle, was responsible for accompanying the dead to the afterlife.

Histories are more full of examples of the fidelity of dogs than of friends.

–Alexander Pope

AESOP'S FABLES

You can't think of fables without thinking of Aesop, a slave who lived in ancient Greece. Most of the fables we know today have been attributed to him, and many of his stories have found their way into popular culture in the form of often-used expressions or metaphors. In his tales, Aesop used a variety of anthropomorphized animals to illustrate his points. Wolves, foxes and even domestic dogs were common characters in his fables.

The Ass's Brains

Lion and Fox went hunting together. Lion, on the advice of Fox, sent a message to Ass, proposing to make an alliance between their two families. Ass came to the place of meeting, overjoyed at the prospect of a royal alliance. But when he arrived, Lion pounced on Ass and said to the Fox: "Here is our dinner for today. Watch you here while I go and have a nap. Woe betide you if you touch my prey." Lion went away, and Fox waited. Finding that his master did not return, Fox ventured to take out the brains of Ass and ate them up. When Lion came back, he soon noticed the absence of the brains and, in a terrible voice, asked Fox, "What have you done with the brains?" Fox replied, "Brains, your Majesty! It had none, or it would never have fallen into your trap."

Moral: Wit has always an answer ready.

Good words by the third time will even bore the dogs.

–Chinese proverb

The Fox and the Leopard

Fox and Leopard disputed which was the more beautiful of the two. Leopard exhibited one by one the various spots that decorated his skin. But the Fox, interrupting him, said, "And how much more beautiful than you am I, who am decorated, not in body, but in mind."

Moral: It is better to be smart than beautiful.

The Fox and the Grapes

This parable is the source of the expression "sour grapes," which is used to describe someone who insults or derides something that he wanted but could not have.

A famished Fox saw some clusters of ripe black grapes hanging from a trellised vine. She resorted to all her tricks to get at them, but wearied herself in vain, for she could not reach them. At last she turned away, hiding her disappointment and saying, "The grapes are sour, and not ripe, as I thought."

Moral: It is easy to dislike that which you cannot have.

The Lion, the Fox and the Beasts

Lion once gave out that he was sick unto death and summoned the animals to come and hear his Last Will and Testament. So Goat came to the Lion's cave and stopped there listening for a long time. Then Sheep went in, and before she came out, Calf came up to receive the last wishes of the Lord of the Beasts. But soon Lion seemed to recover and came to the mouth of his cave, and he saw Fox, who had been waiting outside for some time. "Why do you not come to pay your respects to me?" said Lion to Fox. "I beg your Majesty's pardon," said Fox, "but I noticed the track of the animals that have already come to you. And while I see many hoof marks going in, I see none coming out. Till the animals that have entered your cave come out again, I prefer to remain in the open air."

Moral: It is easier to get into the enemy's toils than out again.

The Lion, the Wolf and the Fox

Lion, growing old, lay sick in his cave. All the beasts came to visit their king, except Fox. Wolf, therefore, thinking that he had a capital opportunity, went to Lion and accused Fox of not paying Lion the respect he deserved, he who had the rule over them all, and of not coming to visit him. At that very moment Fox came in and heard these last words of Wolf. With Lion roaring out in a rage against him, Fox sought an opportunity to defend himself and said, "And who of all those who have come to you have benefited you so much as I, who have traveled from place to place in every direction, and have sought and learnt from the physicians the means of healing you?" Lion commanded him immediately to tell him the cure. Fox replied, "You must flay a wolf alive and wrap his skin, yet warm, around you." Wolf was at once taken and flayed, whereon Fox, turning to him, said with a smile, "You should have moved your master not to ill, but to goodwill."

Moral: Bad things happen to those who stir up ill will.

The Kid and the Wolf

Kid, returning without protection from the pasture, was pursued by Wolf. Seeing he could not escape, he turned round and said: "I know, friend Wolf, that I must be your prey, but before I die, I would ask of you one favor. Will you play me a tune to

which I may dance?" Wolf complied, and while he was piping and Kid was dancing, some Hounds, hearing the sound, ran up and began chasing Wolf. Turning to Kid, he said, "It is just what I deserve; for I, who am only a butcher, should not have turned piper to please you."

Moral: He who steps out of his way to play the fool must not wonder if he misses the prize.

The Shepherd Boy and the Wolf

Shepherd Boy, who watched a flock of sheep near a village, brought out the villagers three or four times by crying out, "Wolf! Wolf!" and when his neighbors came to help him, he laughed at them for their pains. Wolf, however, did truly come at last. Shepherd Boy, now really alarmed, shouted in an agony of terror, "Pray, do come and help me. Wolf is killing the sheep." But no one paid any heed to his cries, nor rendered any assistance. Wolf, having no cause of fear, at his leisure destroyed the whole flock.

Moral: There is no believing a liar, even when he speaks the truth.

The Wolf in Sheep's Clothing

Wolf found great difficulty in getting at the sheep, owing to the vigilance of the shepherd and his dogs. But one day, Wolf found the skin of a sheep that had been flayed and thrown aside, so he put it on over his own pelt and strolled down among the sheep. The Lamb that belonged to the sheep whose skin the Wolf was wearing began to follow the Wolf; so, leading the Lamb a little apart, he soon made a meal of her, and for some time, he succeeded in deceiving the sheep and enjoying hearty meals.

Moral: Appearances can be deceiving.

The Wolf in Sheep's Clothing (a variation)

Some of Aesop's fables had similar themes and characters but were crafted to teach different moral lessons, as you can see from the following fable.

Once upon a time, Wolf resolved to disguise his appearance to secure food more easily. Encased in the skin of a sheep, he pastured with the flock, deceiving the shepherd by his costume. In the evening, he was shut up by the shepherd in the fold; the gate was closed, and the entrance made thoroughly secure. But the shepherd, returning to the fold during the night to obtain meat for the next day, mistakenly caught up the Wolf instead of a sheep and killed him instantly.

Moral: If you look for harm, harm is what you will find.

The Wolf and the Shepherds

Wolf, passing by, saw some Shepherds in a hut eating a haunch of mutton for their dinner. Approaching them, he said, "What a clamor you would raise if I were to do as you are doing!"

Moral: Some condemn in others what they themselves easily do.

The Dog and the Hare

Hound, having startled Hare on the hillside, pursued her for some distance, at one time biting her with his teeth as if he would take her life, and at another fawning upon her, as if in play with another dog. Hare said to him, "I wish you would act sincerely by me and show yourself in your true colors. If you are a friend, why do you bite me so hard? If an enemy, why do you fawn on me?"

Moral: No one can be a friend if you know not whether to trust or distrust him.

The Dog and the Oyster

Dog, used to eating eggs, saw an Oyster and, opening his mouth to its widest extent, swallowed the Oyster down with the utmost relish, supposing it to be an egg. Soon afterwards, suffering great pain in his stomach, Dog said, "I deserve all this torment for my folly in thinking that everything round must be an egg."

Moral: He who acts without sufficient thought will often fall into unsuspected danger.

The Dog and the Shadow

Dog, crossing a bridge over a stream with a piece of flesh in his mouth, saw his own shadow in the water and took it for that of another dog with a piece of meat double his own in size. Dog immediately let go of his own meat and fiercely attacked the other dog to get his larger piece from him. He thus lost both: that which he grasped at in the water, because it was a shadow, and his own, because the stream swept it away.

Moral: If you are greedy, you might lose everything.

The Dog and the Wolf

Wolf was gaunt and almost dead with hunger when he happened to meet a housedog who was passing by. "Ah, Cousin," said Dog. "I know how it would be; your irregular life will soon be the ruin of you. Why do you not work steadily, as I do, and get your food regularly given to you?"

"I have no objection," said Wolf, "if I could only get a place."

"I will easily arrange that for you," said Dog. "Come with me to my master and you shall share my work."

So Wolf and Dog went towards the town together. On the way there, Wolf noticed that the hair on a certain part of Dog's neck was very much worn away and asked how that had come about.

"Oh, it is nothing," said Dog. "That is only the place where the collar is put on at night to keep me chained up. It chafes a bit, but one soon gets used to it."

"Is that all?" said Wolf. "Then good-bye to you, Master Dog."

Moral: Better to starve free than be a fat slave.

The Two Dogs

A man had two dogs: Hound, who was trained to assist him in his sports, and Housedog, taught to watch the house. When he returned home after a good day's sport, the man always gave Housedog a large share of his spoil. Hound, feeling much aggrieved at this, reproached his companion, saying, "It is very hard to have all this labor, while you, who do not assist in the chase, luxuriate on the fruits of my exertions."

Housedog replied, "Do not blame me, my friend, but find fault with the master, who has not taught me to labor but to depend for subsistence on the labor of others."

Moral: Children are not to be blamed for the faults of their parents.

KRASICKI'S FABLES

Although Aesop is the best-known writer of fables, he is not the only writer famous for his moral tales. Ignacy Krasicki, an 18th-century Polish poet, wrote a book of fables entitled Fables and Parables. Like Aesop, Krasicki used anthropomorphized animals in his fables, but his tales had political undertones as well as moral lessons.

Man and Wolf

Man was traveling in wolfskin, when wolf stopped his way.
"Know from my garb," said the man, "what I am, what I may."
The wolf first laughed out loud, then grimly said to the man:
"I know that you are weak, if you need another's skin."

The Wolf and the Sheep

A certain wolf, ever cautious, ravenous withal,
Saw a carcass, advanced and landed in a pitfall.
He sat in the pit, sighing, then all at once heard sheep.
They looked down at the wolf barely breathing in the deep.
At length he spoke, and said with most gentle countenance:
"I didn't fall in, I am down here to do penance—
I'm doing penance for having assaulted, menaced,
For having devoured you…" When the sheep heard this, they asked:
"Come out of the pit!…" "I will not!…" "We will lift you out…"
The wolf demurred but, at the last, yielded to their shout.
The sheep set to work, and so did they set about it,
That ere long they had lifted the wolf out of the pit.
The wolf, rescued from the trap, desired his faith to keep,
And so, slashed, strangled and devoured all the foolish sheep.

DOG WORDS

Dogs play such a huge role in our consciousness that we have even incorporated them into our language.

Bulldogging: a rodeo event in which a rider on horseback chases down a steer and then jumps from the saddle, grabs the steer by the horns and twists its head until it lies on the ground; also known as cattle wrestling.

Cant dog: a lever with a metal spike on one end and pivoting hooked arm, used by lumberjacks to move logs; also known as a "peavey" or "dog hook."

Coydog: a cross between a male coyote and a female domestic dog. (A female coyote/male domestic dog hybrid is called a dogote. Seriously, couldn't scientists come up with better names for these animals?) These hybrids are rare, because coyotes and domestic dogs generally view each other with hostility, not as potential mates. Coydogs and dogotes are thought to be more aggressive and less wary of humans than true coyotes.

Dogbane: a plant from the *Apocynum* genus, which can be found in most temperate regions of the Northern Hemisphere. The plant, which is toxic, is poisonous to dogs, hence the name.

Dogberry: a blundering or incompetent official. In Shakespeare's *Much Ado about Nothing*, Dogberry is the inept police constable, whose buffoonery and constant mangling of the English language provide comic relief in the play.

Dog-eared: a term used to describe something that is worn out or shabby looking, especially a book with pages that are bent over or ragged at the corners.

Dogface: used to describe a soldier, especially in the U.S. infantry in World War II.

Dogfight: an aerial combat between two or more fighter planes. Think Snoopy and the Red Baron.

Dogged: stubbornly persistent.

Doggerel: a short verse of dubious artistic merit.

Doggone: a euphemism for goddamn, as in, "Where did I put my doggone glasses?"

Doggie bag: no one really asks for a doggie bag for their leftovers at restaurants anymore, but the term is still understood. It originally came into popular usage as a euphemistic pretense that allowed diners to take their leftovers home from a restaurant without looking cheap or stingy, by suggesting that the food was for their pet, not for themselves.

Dogleg: a generic term for a sharp bend or turn, specifically, a type of corner on a race track, a feature on a golf course and a style of staircase in which two flights of stairs are positioned at a 90° angle to each other and are joined by a landing.

Dogma: an established belief or tenet of an organization, especially a church, that should never be questioned.

Dog paddle: a swimming style in which the head stays out of the water and the legs kick while the arms are used to pull the body forward. The stroke looks cute when children and dogs do it but is somewhat less dignified when practiced by an adult.

Dogsbody: naval slang for a junior officer who does grunt work. In the early 1800s, sailors called one of their staple foods—a repulsive-looking dish of dried peas boiled in a bag—"dog's body," and the term was soon attached to low-ranking sailors who were stuck doing the tasks no one else wanted to perform.

Dog tags: identification tags, usually two metal disks hanging from a chain around the neck, worn by military personnel. Their main purpose is to identify dead and injured soldiers; one tag always stays with the soldier's body, and the other tag can be snapped off the chain and taken out of the conflict zone, to keep track of casualties left behind.

Dogvane: a nautical term used to describe a light piece of material or bundle of feathers placed on a ship's masthead to indicate the direction of the wind.

Dogwatch: in nautical terms, the period of time from 4:00 PM to 8:00 PM, split into "first dogwatch" (4:00–6:00 PM) and "second dogwatch" (6:00–8:00 PM).

Firedog: a support made of iron or ceramic used in a fireplace to hold the logs off the ground, thereby improving air circulation; also referred to as an andiron. The firedog dates back at least as far as ancient Greece.

Hangdog: gloomy or dejected, as in a hangdog expression on someone's face.

Junkyard dog: used mostly in the U.S., this term is slang for a vicious person who is not to be messed with.

Sundog: a small rainbow that sometimes appears on either side of the sun, when the air is filled with ice crystals or ice fog.

Underdog: a person or team that is expected to lose.

A dog in a kennel barks at his fleas; a dog hunting does not notice them.

–Chinese proverb

DOGGIE EXPRESSIONS

*Not content to have dogs represented only in our words,
we have created expressions that honor (or malign) our
canine companions' characteristics.*

As Sick as a Dog—When someone says, "I'm sick as a dog," it is understood that he or she is suffering from a particularly nasty stomach ailment involving a great deal of throwing up. The first recorded use of this simile dates back to 1705. Why a dog, you ask? Who knows? Maybe "sick as a cat" didn't have the same ring to it.

Barking Up the Wrong Tree—Someone "barking up the wrong tree" is following a wrong line of questioning or reasoning. The expression alludes to the practice of hunting dogs treeing their quarry, then barking at the base of the tree (apparently, sometimes the wrong tree) to let the hunter know where the quarry is hiding.

Call Off the Dogs—To "call off the dogs" means to stop criticizing or harassing someone. The expression is another hunting analogy, in this case referring to a hunter calling his dogs back to him, to stop them from following a scent.

Culture Dog—A person who, to be trendy, tries to weasel his or her way into a culture that he or she has no ties to or understanding of is sometimes called a "culture dog." The term brings to mind a person lingering on the sidelines, panting and vibrating with hopeful anticipation of being accepted, in much the same way a dog acts when it is waiting for you to throw its ball in a rousing game of fetch.

Dog and Pony Show—This phrase is used disparagingly to describe a presentation that is usually for promotional purposes and has more flash than substance. Political campaigns are often referred to as "dog and pony shows" because of the pomp and circumstance that accompany them. Marketing campaigns are also fair game. This phrase seems to have originated in the American Midwest in the late 19th century. It originally had a literal meaning and was used to describe a type of small-scale circus without the means to afford exotic or dangerous animals to draw crowds, relying instead on acts such as clowns, acrobatics and performing dogs and ponies. The expression gradually took on a negative connotation, possibly because larger circuses looked down their collective noses at the smaller organizations. By the 1950s, the expression had lost its literal meaning and taken on the meaning it has today.

Dogs' Breakfast—When I was a kid, my mom used to walk into my bedroom, shake her head in disgust and say, "It looks like a dog's breakfast in here." She didn't mean that I had piles of puppy chow or morsels of meat strewn about; she just meant that the room was a mess. I preferred to think of it as having a "lived-in" look.

(The) Dog's Bullocks—"The cream of the crop," "the bees' knees" and "the dog's bullocks" all have the same general meaning, though which phrase you use depends on the company you keep. "The dog's bullocks" is thought to have originated in England in the late 1980s. Why it is used to denote excellence, when "bullocks" usually has a negative connotation, is anyone's guess. Variations, such as "the pooch's privates" and "the mutt's nuts," are also used across the Pond.

Dog Days of Summer—The "dog days of summer" is used to describe the period between mid-July and mid-August, when temperatures are generally at their hottest. The ancient Romans called the hottest weeks of summer *caniculares dies,* the "days of the dog," in reference to Sirius, the Dog Star. During the "dog days," Sirius, the brightest star in the sky other than the sun, rises at about the same time as the sun, and the Romans believed that the Dog Star was responsible for the oppresive heat and humidity.

A Dog's Dinner—Here's a good question: Why does "a dog's dinner" describe someone who is dressed pretentiously or something designed to attract attention, when "a dog's breakfast" describes a mess? Does a dog's dinner look different from a dog's breakfast? Doesn't it all come from the same bag or can?

Dog-faced Liar—A "dog-faced liar" isn't just your average, run-of-the-mill liar; he or she is the worst kind of liar. Seems a little harsh, though, doesn't it? Most dogs have such cute little faces...

Dog in the Manger—Someone who will not share something that he or she cannot use or does not need is sometimes referred to as a "dog in the manger." The expression comes from Aesop's fable of the same name, in which a dog lies in a manger to take his afternoon nap and prevents an ox from eating the hay, even though he can't eat it himself.

Going to the Dogs—Something "going to the dogs" is degenerating or deteriorating, as in "this planet is going to the dogs." The expression might have emerged as a shortened version of "going to the dog races," which, as any hard-core gambler can tell you, is a path that often leads to ruin.

Hair of the Dog (That Bit You)—An oft-prescribed remedy for a hangover is the "hair of the dog," or the "hair of the dog that bit you," otherwise known as another of the same drink that's making you feel so wretched. The expression alludes to an old folk remedy, in which a person who was bitten by a dog ate one of the offending dog's hairs to ward off negative effects from the bite, such as the onset of infection or rabies.

His Bark is Worse than His Bite—This expression is used to describe someone who seems like a meany but really isn't so bad at all.

In the Doghouse—If you are "in the doghouse," someone is not happy with you. Although the expression can be applied to anyone who has angered someone, it is often used to describe a situation in which a spouse (usually a husband) has done something to annoy his partner and is therefore not welcome in the house (i.e. the bedroom) and must sleep with the dog (i.e. on the couch).

It's a Dog's Life—Some people use this expression to mean that life is easy and relaxed, whereas others use it to mean that life is tough. The origin of the expression is unclear (as, apparently, is its meaning).

Jackalling—"Jackalling" describes a situation in which a person does the grunt work for a senior employee. The expression refers to the fact that jackals sometimes lead a lion to its prey.

Let Sleeping Dogs Lie—This means "do not rehash a topic of conversation that has been settled and will be sure to cause discord if reopened." The oldest known use of this metaphor can be found in Chaucer's *Troilus and Criseyde*, which dates back to 1374, although Chaucer put it somewhat more poetically: "It is nought good a slepyng hound to wake."

Loophole—In the past, when people still traveled on foot and wolves were prevalent in many parts of Europe, stone shelters were set up in isolated areas of the landscape. These huts offered protection in the event that travelers encountered the dreaded canine on their journey. The modern expression "loop hole" is derived from "loup hole" or "wolf hole" and refers to a peephole in the stone wall that allowed a traveler to peek outside and check if the way was clear before leaving the safety of the hut.

Throw Someone to the Wolves—To "throw someone to the wolves" is to sentence someone to a horrible fate or, more realistically, put one in a situation in which he will be heavily criticized or metaphorically torn to pieces. There is a self-serving element to this action, in that the "thrower" usually tosses the "throwee" to deflect attention from himself, thereby saving his own skin. This is another expression for which we have to thank Aesop and his fables. In "The Wolf and the Nurse," the nurse, fed up with her young patient's crying, threatens to toss the child out the window to the awaiting wolf.

Two or Three Dog Night—Indigenous peoples the world over kept dogs as companions and hunting animals, and on especially cold nights, human and canine would hunker together for warmth. The terms "two dog night" and "three dog night" were used to qualify just how cold the temperature was on a particular night. On a "two dog night," a person needed to snuggle with two pooches to stay warm; a "three dog night" called for three dogs.

Why Keep a Dog and Bark Yourself?—This odd little expression means don't pay someone to do something and then do it yourself. You might use this expression for a fastidious homeowner who cleans the house before the maid service comes over.

THE DOGS OF WAR

Using dogs as soldiers in war is not a new concept.
It dates back to ancient Babylonian times, when
Hammurabi's warriors trained dogs to fight alongside
them on the battlefields. The ancient Greeks, Romans
and Persians were all known to use dog soldiers against
their enemies.

A Formidable Canine Opponent

Perhaps the most famous war dogs were those of the Gauls. The Gauls trained their war dogs, huge mastiff-like breeds, to drag enemy soldiers off the backs of horses or out of chariots. The dogs were also trained to attack the horses' legs, to put them out of commission. Gaul war dogs were dressed in chain mail and wore heavy spiked collars to protect their necks.

Enlisted Pooches
In World War I, both sides employed dogs. The German army included more than 30,000 dogs in its force, and France had at least 20,000. Many different breeds were used: collies carried medical supplies to soldiers on the battlefield; Newfoundland dogs, bloodhounds and Irish wolfhounds transported injured soldiers; and terriers delivered cigarettes to soldiers in trenches, kept the trenches rat-free and warmed the sleeping soldiers' feet.

Don't Shoot the Messenger
By about 1917, dogs were widely used as messengers on the battlefields. The courageous pups were fitted with gas masks and respirators, to protect them from the poisonous gas shrouding the combat zone. Some dogs were trained to respond to two handlers and could carry messages back and forth through danger zones. Other dogs were trained to run in only one direction; these dogs had special backpacks carrying pigeons, which flew

messages back to the base. Dogs played such an important role in the Allied forces' strategy that soldiers caught interfering with messenger dogs could face court martial.

British Army Mascot

The British army used Airedales in World War I to carry supplies and locate wounded men. The dogs brought a piece of the injured soldier's clothing back to the camp to alert someone that a soldier was injured. Airedales became the official breed of the British Army.

Look Out Below!

In northern Canada, during World War II, huskies were trained as "parapups," dogs that were dropped from planes (with specially designed parachutes, of course) to rescue survivors of downed military aircraft. Many of the planes that crashed went down in areas with no road access, so the huskies were flown in

and dropped over the site. They wore backpacks full of medical supplies and, when necessary, were used as sled dogs to pull the injured soldiers to safety.

DID YOU KNOW?

During World War II, bloodhounds were used as tracking dogs, but their baying often alerted the enemy, so German shepherds eventually took over their responsibilities.

Jungle Dogs

German shepherds have been used in many wars. They were sentries, guard dogs and attack dogs in both World Wars, and later, in Vietnam, the dogs were used as scouts. Although many other breeds were also used in the Vietnamese jungle, they were unable to handle the heat as well as the German shepherd, which can shed its undercoat, and most dogs of other breeds died of heat stroke.

DID YOU KNOW?

After the Napoleonic wars, Napoleon was given a celebrated veteran poodle, named Moustache, as a gift. The black pooch was trained to raise his leg whenever Napoleon spoke the name of his enemies.

 Jerome Napoleon Bonaparte, the last member of Napoleon's family, died in 1945 of injuries he received after tripping over his dog's leash.

Dogs are not our whole life, but they make our lives whole.
                                        –Roger Caras

RESCUE DOGS

Some of the qualities that we most value in our canine companions are their generous spirits and their willingness to "lend a paw" to a person in need. Rescue dogs put these qualities to good use.

Dogpaddling Life Savers

In Italy and France, Newfoundland dogs have been trained and employed as lifeguards for years, and other European nations are starting to do the same. The United Kingdom recognized its first fully qualified Newfoundland dog lifeguard in 2007—the dog rescues struggling bathers from the rough waters of Cornwall.

Seek and Ye Shall Find

A dog's keen sense of smell is one of its greatest assets, and it is one of the reasons the animal is so valued by search and rescue (SAR) teams. SAR dogs are put to various uses, each responsibility requiring a different type of training. Some of the jobs SAR dogs perform include:

- airscenting—these dogs are not trained to search for a specific person but to locate any person in a specific area; they are often used to search places in which criminals are thought to be hiding, or for victims that might be in the area but are not immediately visible

- avalanche rescue— these dogs are trained to locate people buried under snow and to begin digging the victim out; they can dig to depths of about ¾ of their body length before their handlers have to take over

- cadaver search—I think the name says it all, really

- disaster rescue—does not search for a specific individual but tries to pick up any scent possible and rescues people in "unnatural terrain," such as collapsed buildings; these dogs were used to find people buried in the twin towers after 9–11

☛ tracking—these dogs search for a specific person on a fresh trail, without requiring the use of an article of clothing or personal item to pick up the scent

☛ trailing—this dog needs to sniff something with a person's scent on it to pick up the trail of a particular individual on a cold trail; once the dog has a scent article, it can follow the trail over natural landscapes

☛ water recovery—these dogs usually work from a boat and are trained to locate any human scent in the water; they are usually more effective for recovery than for actual rescue

SNIFFER DOGS

SAR dogs are not the only canines prized for their scenting abilities. Sniffer dogs provide valuable services for many government agencies, police forces and private companies. These dogs are trained to detect all kinds of things, including archaeological remains, arson and accelerants, bedbugs, bombs, counterfeit currency, dry rot, endangered species, gas leaks, landmines, mold, narcotics, pirated CDs and DVDs, termites and weapons. Sniffer dogs are also used to detect illnesses such as hyperglycemia in people with diabetes and different types of cancer.

Something Smells Funny

In 2006, sniffer dogs working with Canadian border service officers helped their handlers make more than 540 seizures of counterfeit money, totaling 12.9 million dollars. The dogs can detect the "funny money" by the high concentrations of ink that it contains.

Bits of red herring were often spread on a trail to throw off tracking dogs, hence the expression "red herring" used to describe a misleading clue.

Busted!

In the U.S., customs and border officers credit their sniffer dogs with helping them make more than 6000 arrests annually; most were people trying to cross the border with weapons, drugs or counterfeit currency.

Watch Where You Step

Dogs are currently being used in more than 30 countries around the world to detect land mines, trip wires and other unexploded ordinance. Trained to sniff out TNT or metallic wiring, dogs are three times more effective than any machinery currently being used for the same purpose. Land mine-detecting dogs have been put to work in such countries as Angola, Azerbaijan, Bosnia, Colombia, Costa Rica, Croatia, Mozambique, Nicaragua and Rwanda, to name a few, and they are currently playing an important role in Afghanistan and Iraq. Recently, mine-detecting dogs have been replaced by mine-detecting rats in a few countries, including Mozambique, Zimbabwe and Cambodia. The rodents also have a well-developed sense of smell but are less expensive and, unlike dogs, are not heavy enough to set off the mines if they step on them.

Be proud but not arrogant. Be beautiful but not vain.
Be strong but gentle. Be loving, be humble, be as much
like a dog as you can....

–Trixie Koontz (a.k.a. Dean Koontz)

POLICE DOGS

A dog's natural agility, intelligence and fearlessness make it a good candidate for K-9 training. Canine police officers work side by side with their human handlers to keep the streets safe for the rest of us.

I'll Take You Down!

A police dog's primary responsibility is to chase down suspects and hold them captive until its handler gets there. I'm sure everyone has seen dramatic footage of a police dog taking down a fleeing suspect, and we have probably all cringed a little with inadvertent sympathy when the criminal hit the pavement with 135 pounds (60 kilograms) of snarling dog attached to his arm. Although the dogs are not trained to hurt suspects, they are trained to hold onto their captives at all cost, and they sometimes inflict a great deal of injury in the process. Police dogs are also useful for intimidation—sometimes, just knowing a dog will be set on him convinces a criminal to surrender. Throw in a few bared teeth and a menacing growl, and even the toughest bad guy is likely to think twice before bolting.

 DOG FACT Every dog's noseprint is unique and can be used for identification, much like fingerprints are for people. All dogs that are bonded, such as security dogs, must have their noseprints on file.

Multi-purpose Pups

Police forces also use their four-legged officers as sniffer dogs, especially for narcotics, explosives, weapons and cadavers. In North America, some police forces employ crisis response dogs—dogs that are brought in to sit with victims and provide comfort, especially to traumatized children. Newfoundland dogs are one of the most commonly used breeds for crisis response dogs, probably because they look like giant, cuddly stuffed animals. Okay, I suppose it could also be because they are known for being gentle creatures, especially with kids.

DID YOU  **KNOW?**

Police dogs are actual police officers, and shooting a police dog is a felony in many countries.

> *Beware of the man who does not talk*
> *and the dog that does not bark.*
>
> –Cheyenne proverb

DRAFT ANIMALS

Although it is not often seen these days, at one time dogs were commonly put to use hauling heavy loads.

Ox, Shmox—I've Got a Dog

Some of the bigger dog breeds, including the Newfoundland dog and the Rottweiler, were used as draft animals in Europe into the 20th century. They pulled such things as milk carts, wagons full of butchered meat and buggies full of packages and letters for the postal service, among other things. During the World Wars, these dogs were even used as the first powered wheelchairs, hauling wounded soldiers around in wagons until the soldiers were strong enough to get around without help.

DID YOU  KNOW?

The Newfoundland dog can haul weights as much as 25 times heavier than its own body weight.

Mush!

When we think of the Arctic, one of the first images to come to mind is that of a pack of dogs pulling a sled across the frozen landscape. Although sled dogs are used largely for recreation these days, they still play a vital role in the survival of northern peoples; the Inuit have relied on sled dogs for centuries. In the days before helicopters and snowmobiles, dog sleds were the only transportation for crossing the vast stretches of Arctic ice and snow, other than on foot. Some of the most common breeds of sled dog include the Siberian husky, the Alaskan Malamute and the Qimmiq (also known as the Canadian Eskimo dog).

The Iditarod

One of the most famous dog sled races is the Iditarod, whose route stretches from Anchorage to Nome, Alaska, following the path taken by the dog sled teams in the famous Great Race of Mercy, the 1925 serum run that delivered diphtheria antitoxin to Nome. First run in 1973, the Iditarod takes place every March and usually lasts from 10 to 15 days.

DID YOU KNOW?

Sled dogs running the Iditarod burn an average of 10,000 calories a day.

This Would be a Lot Easier with Snow

Northern cultures were not the only ones to use dogs for transporting goods. Before they had horses, many Native Americans on the prairies and plains hooked dogs up to travois to haul loads over land. A travois was a sled made from two poles tied together at one end, to form an isosceles triangle. Netting was strung between the two poles, and the dog was harnessed to the narrow end of the triangle. Goods to be transported were piled onto the netting.

Dogs often bury food that is too hard to for them to eat, because it softens while it is in the ground.

ASSISTANCE DOGS

Because they are highly intelligent, social animals, dogs have become invaluable companions to people with special needs. Assistance dogs are more than just pets; they are the eyes, ears and even hands and feet of people whose senses or bodies do not work as well as they should. Legally speaking, assistance dogs have special status and can accompany their handlers into areas in which pet dogs are not allowed.

Let Me Be Your Guide

Guide dogs, often (incorrectly) called seeing eye dogs, have been used since the end of World War I to lead individuals with impaired vision. The dogs are trained to use "intelligent disobedience," which means they are expected to refuse their handlers' orders if they deem them to be unsafe. For example, if a handler asks his dog to move forward, but the dog sees a car coming, it is expected to ignore the handler's instruction.

Guide dogs not only have to watch for ground obstacles, such as parking meters, lamp posts, and pedestrians, they also have to keep an eye open for overhead obstacles, such as low-hanging awnings and tree limbs. The most common breeds used as guide dogs are German shepherds, Labrador retrievers and golden retrievers.

Furry, Four-legged Hearing Aids

Hearing dogs are paired with deaf handlers and are trained to let their handlers know if the phone rings, a baby is crying, the oven timer goes off, or if they have dropped their keys on the sidewalk—any auditory cue that the handler cannot pick up on without help. On the street, these dogs must warn their handlers if they hear an emergency vehicle siren—they even have to indicate from which direction the siren is coming. I gotta say, I could use a little help with that last task myself.

At Your Service

Service dogs are trained to help people with limited mobility perform tasks they cannot do for themselves. These dogs can perform an astonishing variety of jobs, including unloading the dryer, unpacking groceries, fetching items from the fridge, calling 911 on a K-9 phone, removing people's clothing, pulling blankets up or down for bedridden patients and even moving paralyzed limbs back into the proper position on a wheelchair if they get knocked askew.

A Fisherman's Best Friend

Newfoundland dogs have long been popular aboard fishing ships. They help fishermen pull in their nets and retrieve items (and people) that fall overboard. In the past, Newfoundland dogs also swam from ship to ship with correspondence.

On the Hunt

Humans have capitalized on canine hunting skills since the lives of dogs and humans first became intertwined. In fact, many people believe that this is the main reason the dog was first domesticated. Many different kinds of hunting dogs have been bred, but they can be lumped into four main categories:

1. Hounds
- ☞ sighthounds—these dogs track their prey visually, then chase it down and kill it

- ☞ scenthounds—these breeds track their prey by its scent; they often hunt in packs and usually tree their quarry, instead of killing it

2. Gun dogs
- ☞ retrievers—these dogs collect the game after the hunter has killed it

- ☞ water dogs—a subclass of retrievers, these dogs swim out to get birds that are shot over water

- ☞ pointers—these breeds indicate where game is hiding, so the hunter can shoot it

- ☞ setters—are similar to pointers but are used exclusively to hunt birds and flush the game when the hunter is close enough to shoot it

- ☞ spaniels—can be used for birds and small mammals and are similar to setters in that they flush the prey when the hunter is within shooting range

3. Terriers—used mostly for hunting burrowing animals, often by digging the quarry out of its den

4. Curs—similar to terriers but are used to hunt larger animals, such as raccoons and cougars

Duck Wranglers

In Kojen, Holland, waterfowl hunters had a rather unique method of the catching ducks. They dug a long trench out of a pond in which ducks congregated then strung a net over the trench. The hunter's Kooikerhondje then set to frolicking on the shore, to attract the attention of the ducks. The curious ducks were drawn by the dog's antics into the trench, under the overhanging net. The net blocked escape by flight, while the hunter and dog blocked the end of the trench, so the whole flock was captured in one fell swoop. Conservation officers still use this method for catching ducks they want to band or relocate.

You Don't Scare Me!

It takes a special kind of dog to confront a grizzly bear, but that's exactly what Karelian bear dogs are trained to do. These aggressive, courageous dogs are helping to keep both bears and humans safe in areas where the two species coexist. When a bear wanders into an area with a lot of human activity, chances are good that someone will get hurt (and that someone is most often the bear). In these situations, wildlife officers sometimes use Karelian bear dogs to track the bear and drive it out of the area, back into the wilderness where it belongs.

Home, Home on the Range

Herding dogs are not expected to protect a flock from predators; these dogs help the rancher round up the flock, usually by nipping the livestock in the heels, or by "staring down" the animals, driving the stock where the rancher wants them to go. Guarding dogs, on the other hand, bond with the flock they oversee and protect it from potential predators. These dogs are usually introduced into their flock when they are just young pups, usually only a few weeks old, so that they will imprint on the animals they are in charge of protecting.

Performing Pups

Turn on your TV any given night and, chances are, you will see dog actors on the screen. They star in movies, TV shows and in all types of commercials, even those advertising non-pet related products. The popularity of dogs on the small and big screen has given rise to animal talent agencies—Is your dog the next Lassie?—and even doggie actors' guilds.

You Look Mahvelous...
And we mustn't forget doggie models. Someone's got to make those overpriced leashes and collars look good.

Circus Stars
The Wow Wow Dog Circus from Hong Kong claims to be the largest of its kind in the world. Its more than 100 dogs are trained to perform a variety of tricks, including acrobatics, tightrope walking, rope skipping and trapeze swinging. The dogs are dressed in brightly colored costumes and wear heavy makeup for their performances. In 2005, the circus set a Guinness World Record with 53 jump rope skips by 10 dogs.

DID YOU  **KNOW?**

In the not-so-distant past, before hygiene held as much importance as it does today, the well-to-do would carefully tuck their little lap dogs into bed at night before retiring themselves—not out of concern for the pooches' comfort, but so that bed bugs and fleas would feed on the dog and leave their owners alone.

 A dog is considered to be geriatric when it has lived three-quarters of its life expectancy.

CANINE COUTURE

*The world of fashion is not just for humans anymore.
Pretty much any product that you can imagine purchasing for yourself can be created for your pampered pup.*

What Today's Dog is Wearing

I realize that there are practical reasons for putting clothes on your dog, especially if it is one of the smaller breeds—a sweater, perhaps, for a little pooch whose fur is too thin to protect it from harsh winter weather, or booties to protect its feet from snowy or ice-covered pavement—but really, there is such a thing as taking it too far. Consider the following:

designer jackets with real fur linings

sheepskin bomber jackets

raincoats

snowsuits

scarves and hats

a collar and tie, for a more formal occasion

tuxedos

wedding dresses

UV sunsuits with matching sunhats

swimwear, including bikinis, tankinis and board shorts

beach shorts

sunglasses

velour tracksuits

helmets

bathrobes

PJs with matching slippers

(I swear, I am not making this up!)

But, why stop there? Wouldn't little Princess look fab in a white, rose-adorned tutu, or a little black party dress? Or how about a tennis dress or yellow sundress, complete with matching sunhat. And for your manly dog, nothing says "macho" like a fringed, biker dog scarf (which, by the way, looks alarmingly like a triangular-shaped, black leather hula skirt). That'll make him look tough! All these products are available online, and some of them will set you back a pretty penny, depending on the size of your dog. Don't be surprised to find yourself shelling out a little more for the therapy sessions your pooch will need to recover from the inevitable mocking he or she gets from the other neighborhood dogs.

Boo (Hoo Hoo)

I wonder how pets feel about Halloween. The doorbell rings throughout the evening. Hordes of strange children pack onto the front step. Prowling around are scary-looking creatures that smell human but look much, much different. It's probably

enough to completely stress out a dog with a more sensitive nature. But, just in case it isn't, we can now add pet costumes to the fun. In North America, pets are often considered members of the family; so, the thinking seems to be, why shouldn't they partake in Halloween festivities? The range of costumes available for Fido is astonishing— from your basic vampire cape or devil horns headband to elaborate, full body costumes, such as knight's armor, a giant hot dog (complete with bun and toppings) and Darth Vader or Princess Leia. You can even dress your dog like another animal, say, a skunk or a frog. Hmmmm…would dressing up your pooch like a cat be considered cruel and unusual punishment?

Everything in Its Place

Once you've picked out all the outfits you plan to inflict upon your unsuspecting pooch, you need somewhere to keep them, right? You can't expect to hang them in your closet alongside your own wardrobe. That would be silly. The obvious solution, then, is a doggie armoire, in which you can hang all of your pooch's latest fashions. These armoires look much like ones you might buy for a child but smaller, with much, much smaller hangers. They are also doggie themed, with features such as bone-shaped handles and hangers decorated with little doggie paw prints.

Let's Not Forget Footwear

Again, I can understand a practical need for doggie footwear. Well, for some dogs, anyway, such as the toy breeds or those that spend a lot of time outside in nasty weather. So, winter booties I can get behind. Even hiking boots make sense…sort of. Running shoes might be treading a fine line between useful and ridiculous. But bunny slippers? Black or white rhinestone cowdog boots? Enough said.

DOG FACT

A great deal of the "faux" fur used in the fashion industry and to create those little, fur-covered animal figures sold in Chinese stores and tourist places is actually dog fur. Factories in China slaughter raccoon dogs, as well as domestic dogs, including German shepherds and Dobermans, for their coats. Many animal welfare groups worldwide have investigated the industry and have condemned it as inhumane because of the barbaric methods used to kill the animals.

Accessorize, Accessorize, Accessorize

Just picking out the perfect wardrobe for your pet is not enough. Everyone knows that it's the accessories that make or break an outfit. And boy, are there a lot of accessories to choose from! If jewelry is FiFi's thing, she can choose from diamond-encrusted collars, with or without the matching leash; bone- or tiara-shaped fur clips (also known as barrettes); charms for collars; personalized necklaces; and even anklets. If Fido isn't into shiny trinkets, he can indulge in plenty of other accessories, including bandanas, baseball caps and backpacks.

If you are a dog and your owner suggests that you wear a sweater...suggest that he wear a tail.

–Fran Lebowitz

PAMPERED POOCH PRODUCTS

An entire industry is built up around the love pet owners have for the furry members of the family. The range and creativity of the products marketed to dog lovers boggle the mind. Some ideas, however, are better than others.

It's All Biodegradable

Responsible dog owners clean up after their pets, and that usually involves the lowly plastic bag. The problem with this method, though, is that bagging your dog's mess in plastic prevents a normally biodegradable product (the poop) from breaking down, and you end up with piles of excrement-filled baggies just sitting in a landfill. The solution? Biodegradable poop bags. Relatively new to the market, but apparently catching on, these bags decompose along with their contents, so they can be thrown into a compost heap, buried or picked up with your other organic waste. Now that's a good idea!

Safety First

The first thing most people do when getting into a car is buckle up. Wouldn't want to go flying through the windshield if the car crashes, now, would we? Pet owners concerned with their pets suffering the same fate can rest a little easier knowing that a variety of canine car safety products are available. Doggie car seats come in many forms, but the general theme is a kennel or travel bag with a strap that goes around the headrest to anchor the bag to the seat of the car. Doggie seat belts are basically harnesses with leashes that wrap around the back of the seat. For smaller dogs, there are booster seats, which look a little like hanging flower planters, except that they are slightly wider and attach to the top of the passenger seat instead of to a windowsill. The boosters allow your pet to see comfortably out the window without having to stand on the seat, wobbling and bracing his paws on the dashboard or doorframe. The elevated platform is roomy enough for your petite pup to curl up, and a harness attached to the seat keeps the little guy safe.

Chew on This

I'm sure there are many people who would like to bite George Bush's head off. Or Dick Cheney's. Or Osama bin Laden's, for that matter. Well, while we might never have the satisfaction, literally chewing someone's head off is possible for our pooches. A line of political chew toys has been created that includes a variety of world leaders and other newsworthy figures of debatable popularity. Figures in the series include Hillary Clinton, Mahmoud Ahmadinejad, Michael Moore, Kim Jong-il and Tony Blair. So, next time one of Bush's policies pisses you off, toss his likeness to your pup and sit back to enjoy the show.

SPF 40 for Me, Please

I can't decide if canine sunscreen should be considered a useful pet care product, or if it is one of those people-will-buy-any-thing-type rip-offs. At first reckoning, sunscreen for dogs seems a little frou frou, but with the way the ozone layer is heading, perhaps your pup should be protected from damaging UV rays—especially if it's a hairless breed. So, for me, the jury is still out on this one. As for matching sunglasses for you and your pet? Blech.

Why Fifi, You Look Divine!

I'm not sure why you would ever feel the need to dye your beloved pup's fur, but should you feel such an inclination, you'll be happy to know that there is actually a fur dye on the market. The color choice is somewhat limited, so you'll have to make do with either pink or blue. If you think your pup is still looking a little drab, you can always spruce up her nails with a nice coat of puppy polish, also available. Let's hope the polishes are non-toxic; you wouldn't want Princess to lick the polish off in an attempt to do herself in and reclaim a little canine credibility.

DID YOU KNOW?

As proof that the world of show dogs can be slightly bizarre, I offer the existence of canine under-eye concealer. This product is used on show dogs with white fur to hide blemishes and staining caused by tears. What's next? Lipstick?

A Quick Fix

Hollywood must have dreamed up this product. Only the movie industry is silly enough to envision a product that you can spray on dog stool to freeze it for easier clean up. Yup, that's right. Just point the can at the pile, push the spray nozzle and…voila! Frozen dog doo. Then, you can just pick up the frosty mess and toss it into the garbage. No muss, no fuss.

Watch Where You Point that Thing!

And how about a spring action pooper scooper? Just squeeze the handle and the jaws shoot forward to engulf the pile. With a second handle squeeze, the jaws shoot forward again and dump the mess into the receptacle of your choosing. I shudder to think of the frightening potential for a mishap with this product. Things could go horribly wrong, especially if combined with the freezing spray...

 At least one million dogs in the U.S. have been named the primary beneficiary in their owner's wills. I'll bet that sits well with the rest of the owners' families.

Eau de Toilette

I get dog shampoo. I might even be able to wrap my head around doggie conditioner. Who doesn't like soft locks? But I've gotta draw the line at canine spritz and perfume. I admit, wet dog is not a pleasant smell, but have we learned nothing since Elizabethan times? Perfume does not remove odors; it just covers them up! Speaking of odors, you can also buy doggie breath freshener sprays and breath strips.

Money will buy you a pretty good dog,
but it won't buy the wag of his tail.

–Author Unknown

DOGGIE SERVICES

The pet industry is not just dedicated to creating products for owners to spoil their furry companions with; it has also delved into creating a range of services little Fifi simply can't do without. Again, some services have more merit than others.

Under the Knife

What do you get for the puppy that has everything? How about plastic surgery? A vet in Sao Paolo, Brazil, has adapted common plastic surgery techniques to use on Fido. He reshapes and straightens ears, gives Botox injections to fix inverted eyelashes and has even tightened droopy teats. According to the vet, beauty is important to the animal's wellbeing, because an attractive dog has a better relationship with its owner. Some owners must agree, because the trend is gaining popularity in Brazil, the U.S. and Europe. Nothing says "I love you" like gratuitous surgery.

Open Wide

Many parents would beam with pride if their child chose to study orthodontics. Orthodontics for humans, that is. But how about doggie orthodontics? Does that carry with it the same parental bragging rights? It's gotta look a little strange on a business card. A few dedicated souls are seeing to it that our canine pals are no longer limited to the kind of dentistry that the average veterinarian performs, such as teeth cleaning or tooth extraction. Now our orthodontally challenged pooches can reap the benefits of root canals, crowns, retainers and braces. They can even have a pronounced overbite corrected. The price of doggie orthodontics is on par with its human counterpart, but not many people are qualified to work on dogs—there are only about 70 certified veterinary orthodontists worldwide.

Are You Gonna Use That Kidney?

For some dogs, kidney failure no longer has to be a death sentence; they can now get a kidney transplant. In the U.S., approximately 1000 such transplants are done every year. However, before you sign Fido up for his operation, there are a couple of considerations. The first? Cost. At upwards of US$10,000 per surgery, few owners can afford the hefty price tag. The second? Ethics. The practice is highly controversial, because the donor dog cannot give consent and its life is put at risk; it also suffers a great deal of pain from a completely unnecessary surgery. Often, the donors are strays. A pet owner whose dog undergoes such a surgery is expected to adopt the donor animal after it recovers, but the bottom line is that the surgery puts one life at risk to prolong another, which doesn't sit well with many animal lovers. Also, the transplant surgery only adds about two years to the ailing dog's life. Still, when a beloved pet is suffering, it is only natural for an owner to do whatever it takes to make it feel better. Canine kidney transplants are on the rise in the U.S.

Dog Paddle Your Way to Health

The health benefits of swimming have been well documented, so it is not surprising that swim therapy is available for your ailing pooch. The dogs swim in a heated pool with a trained therapist, who helps them increase their range of motion and strengthen their muscles. The most commonly treated problems include arthritis, hip dysplasia and recovery from knee surgery, but even healthy dogs can benefit from the treatments. The no-impact workout improves muscle tone without straining the dog's joints.

A Little to the Left

Dog massage, also known as canine myofunctional therapy, is another piece of the alternative healing pie of pet care. The benefits dogs reap from massage are similar to those we humans experience—relaxation, increased mobility and, according to canine massage practitioners, a happier state of mind. Massage by a trained professional can help speed an injured dog's recovery and has even been credited with improving the behavior of problem dogs. But the practice not only has a healing role, it can also be used to screen dogs for looming health issues. Canine massage therapists are trained to watch for lumps, changes in fur or other symptoms that suggest an ailment is lurking undiagnosed in the dog's body.

Somepuppy to Love

If your pooch is looking a little down in the muzzle because he needs a little canine company, he's in luck, because there is now such a thing as an online dating agency for dogs. This service helps you track down other dogs to breed with your pet, set up puppy play dates, organize group walks or find a new home for a pet in need.

Have Your Cake and Eat It, Too

Who doesn't love walking into the local bakery and inhaling the intoxicating scents of freshly baked treats? Your pup would probably feel the same should he wander into one of the many doggie bakeries popping up around the nation. These bakeries specialize in dog treats that look good enough for owners to eat (and many are in fact suitable for human consumption). The products contain all-natural ingredients, which makes them healthier for your pet than the treats offered in supermarkets. You can order cakes or cookies to celebrate a Best in Show placing, a graduation and, of course, a birthday, or to welcome a new pup into the family.

DOG FACT In humans, most allergic reactions take the form of respiratory symptoms; allergic reactions in dogs almost always show up on the skin.

DID YOU KNOW?

At least one company in the U.S. has an innovative take on the traditional greeting card—theirs are edible. The cards are specifically for dogs and are made of rawhide printed with non-toxic ink. You can choose from birthday, get well soon, welcome and "just because" cards.

Not Enough Quality Time

A first glance, enrolling your pooch in doggie daycare might seem a little decadent. Is it really necessary, you might ask. After all, we are talking about a dog, not a child. Well, doggie daycare may not be as superfluous as you'd think. With the fast pace of modern life, many people do not have enough time to properly meet the needs of their furry, four-legged friends. The result is an unhappy, sometimes neurotic, dog with behavioral problems. Because dogs are pack animals, they do not do well when left too much by themselves. Doggie daycare provides them with the opportunity to interact with other dogs, as well as humans. The dog is happy because it gets a little company and some mental stimulation while its owners are out, and the owners get to ease their guilty conscience for leaving their pooch alone all day. This leaves them free to focus on more important things, like earning piles of money, which they can use to buy back their pup's affection. Those gourmet puppy treats don't come cheap, you know....

If you stop every time a dog barks,
your road will never end.

–Saudi Arabian proverb

RUFF TREATMENT

Dogs may be pampered pets in North America, but they don't have it so easy in other parts of the world. Many wander the street, hungry and homeless, never knowing when they might get their next meal. And those are the lucky ones...

Free to a Good Home

Spanish newspapers are full of photos of scrawny, sad-eyed pups found dumped on the roadside or living in abandoned buildings and needing a good home. People drop their unwanted dogs off in the traffic circles in the mistaken belief that someone will see the animals and take them in. More often than not, the dogs are just struck and killed by vehicles. Those that are a little more traffic savvy exist on the edge of starvation, every rib and vertebrae showing through their skin as they scour the landscape for garbage or scarf down the scraps thrown to them by compassionate strangers.

Olympic Shame

Things are no better in Greece, home to a staggering number of stray dogs. A common method of keeping their populations in check, especially in rural areas, is to set out poisoned bait food. The country received worldwide attention in 2004 when, just in time for the Summer Olympics, thousands of stray dogs were poisoned in Athens. The government of Greece was accused of killing the dogs to remove them from the public eye before tourists started flooding into the city to attend the games. The government denied the allegations, but that did not stop the global cry of outrage at such callous treatment of "man's best friend."

You Dirty Dog, You

In the Middle East, dogs generally do not enjoy the same pampered status they hold in many Western countries. In fact, strict Muslims consider dogs filthy animals. Although there is no reference in the Koran to dogs being unclean, this attitude has been deeply etched into the Islamic belief system. However, it is slowly changing in some Middle Eastern countries, as younger generations become more interested in trying their hand at pet ownership.

You're Under Arrest

In what has to be one of the strangest stories to hit the wires in a while, in 2002, an Iranian cleric named Hojatolislam Hassani called for his government to arrest all dogs. Hassani was quoted as saying, "Because they are unclean, I demand the judiciary arrest of all dogs with long, medium or short legs—together with their long-legged owners." Hassani was particularly concerned that dog ownership was a sign of the "corrupting influence of decadent Western Culture." And someone in the Iranian government must have agreed with him. In June 2002, the sale of dogs was banned throughout the country, and anyone caught walking a dog in public was fined. Although dogs are generally considered unclean in the Islamic faith, dog ownership is on the rise in Iran, especially in Tehran, among the wealthier classes.

You Call That a Sport?

It's undeniable that many of the events held by the ancient Romans in their amphitheatres were senseless and bloody. One popular, and incredibly cruel, example is bear-baiting, in which a bear was pitted against a number of dogs, to see which animal emerged victorious. Unfortunately, this blood sport did not die out with the fall of the Roman Empire. It was still popular in England during Shakespeare's time and was only made illegal in Britain in 1835. Today, though technically illegal, bear-baiting is still relatively common in Pakistan. It may no longer be held in a Roman amphitheatre, but it is still as violent and bloody as it ever was. The bear is attached to a chain to limit its mobility and prevent it from running away, and its claws and teeth are usually torn out before it faces the dogs. Even so, it still inflicts devastating damage on the dogs, as they slowly tear it to pieces. Many of the dogs used in bear-baiting (usually bull terriers) die of their injuries, even if they succeed in killing the bear.

Dog Beat Dog

Although it is illegal in many countries, dog fighting is still a reality across the globe. In North America, dog fighting is against the law, and it is a felony throughout most of the U.S., but instead of putting an end to the practice, banning it has simply pushed it underground. More often than not, the blood sport is linked with organized crime. The dogs are trained to be vicious and then are pitted against each other in the ring, usually fighting until one of them kills the other. A word of warning to pet owners: fighting dogs are trained for the ring by having them kill smaller bait animals—often stolen pets or animals from "free to a good home" ads in the newspaper.

England was the first country to ban dog fighting. The blood sport has been illegal in the UK since the Cruelty to Animals act of 1835. However, as with Canada and the U.S., outlawing the practice has merely pushed it underground, and it is still common in rural areas.

In Japan, dog fighting dates back to the days of the Samurai and is still an accepted part of the culture. In this more genteel form of the blood sport, the dogs do not fight to the death. Instead, the battle is a timed event, much like a boxing match. A veterinarian watching from the sidelines can put a stop to the fight if it gets out of hand and a dog is badly injured. Having said that, it is still a blood sport, and the dogs are still trained to tear at each other. The most common breed of fighting dog in Japan is the Tosa.

Mutt on the Menu

In China, some dog breeds—chow chows, for example—are raised on farms for their hides and their meat. Dog fur is used in China's fashion industry and is mostly found in trim and glove linings. In fact, what is often labeled "faux fur" is actually dog or cat fur. Dog meat was once a staple for many Chinese people, and restaurants serving dog meat were plentiful. This is slowly changing in China, with dogs becoming more common as cherished pets rather than main courses, but the meat can still be ordered in many restaurants, and dogs are sold in markets alongside other livestock destined for the soup pot.

Poshintang, or dog meat soup, is a popular summertime food in Korea. It is thought to have a number of health benefits, including enhancing male virility, clearing women's complexions and alleviating heat-related illnesses.

Dog meat is also eaten in a number of African countries, including South Africa, the Congo, Zimbabwe and Nigeria. In Nigeria, the meat is thought to improve one's sex life and

provide protection from many diseases, poisons and *juju* (charms). In Abuja, Nigeria, dog meat is so widely consumed that dogs are becoming rare in the town, and pet dogs often go "missing" from their yards.

Before you say to yourself, "Eating dog meat? Ugh. It can't happen in North America," let me assure you that it can, and it does. In Mexico, many indigenous cultures believed the Xoloitzcuintle had special healing qualities, and the unlucky pooch was eaten during religious rituals and for medicinal purposes. Even today, "Xolo" meat is still consumed in rural areas and can be found for sale in local markets.

Nip and Tuck

Ever wonder why a Doberman's ears are so perky? It's because a veterinarian has shaped them to look that way. Some dog breeds, such as Dobermans, Great Danes and schnauzers, routinely have their ears cropped to conform to the breed standard set by kennel clubs. The dogs are put under anesthetic, usually when they are 10 to 14 weeks old, and their ears are cut to the accepted shape and then taped until they are trained to stay that way.

Some breed standards also call for a dog's tail to be cut off (docked). Rottweilers, Dobermans, Jack Russell terriers and boxers are a few breeds whose tails are subject to docking. In this process, the puppy (usually between three and five days old) is *not* given anesthetic before its tail is sliced off with a scalpel or snipped off with scissors. Badly docked tails can cause spinal injuries and chronic skin problems for dogs.

The practice of cropping and docking might have originated to prevent working dogs from getting injured when their ears and tail tips snagged in brush or brambles. However, once people got used to seeing the breeds in their modified condition, the surgical alterations became commonplace, even for pets that would never be expected to work a day in their lives. But attitudes are slowly changing. In Canada, cropping is banned in Newfoundland and Labrador, and the Canadian Veterinary Medical Association has taken a stand against both docking and cropping, with many vets refusing to perform the surgeries. Many European countries, including Austria, Belgium, and France, have banned both practices outright, while other countries, such as Australia, New Zealand and Israel, have banned cosmetic cropping and docking, although the surgeries can still be performed by vets if there is a valid medical reason. Some nations, such as Denmark and Germany, have banned cropping and docking for most breeds but still allow the procedure to be carried out on gun dog breeds, if the animals are working dogs.

DOG LAWS

"While you live under my roof, you live by my rules," is a phrase I'm sure we have all heard countless times while growing up (usually uttered through grinding teeth, at least in my case). A similar expression could be applied to our cuddly canine companions—just replace "under my roof" with "in this community."

Banned in Beijing

Until 1996, it was illegal to own a pet dog in Beijing. Since the ban was lifted, dog ownership has really taken off, with more than one million pet dogs registered in the city by 2006. Not all dogs are welcome, however. Breeds standing 14 inches (35 centimeters) or more at the shoulder are still banned in central Beijing, which means that two of the most popular dogs in China, the Siberian husky and the Labrador retriever, are actually considered illegal breeds in that city.

Puppy Profiling

Because of their use in dog fighting, many breeds have been labeled aggressive, unpredictable and a threat to the general public. As a result, Breed Specific Legislation (BSL) was born. BSL has been called the "canine equivalent of racial profiling," because it judges all dogs by breed, not by individual personality. Under this legislation, ownership of certain dog breeds is restricted or banned outright. BSL exists in many countries, sometimes on a federal level and other times on a more local basis.

In August 2005, Ontario officially banned the breeding, selling, purchasing and importing of American pit bulls and Staffordshire terriers, as well as any dog similar in appearance to the two breeds. Anyone owning one of these breeds before

August 29, 2005, could keep the dog, as long as it was sterilized, registered and muzzled when in a public place.

The UK's Dangerous Dog Act of 1991 made it a criminal offence to own a breed deemed dangerous. This includes the Tosa, the Dogo Argentino and the Fila Brasiliero, or any dog similar in appearance. From the time the act was passed until 1997, police officers in the UK had the authority to seize and destroy any dog of the banned breed "type," meaning any dog that looked like one of the banned breeds. To have a dog returned, owners were required to prove that their dog was not a restricted breed type, a near-impossible task, considering how closely some breeds resemble each other. In 1997, the act was changed to allow the courts to decide on a case-by-case basis whether a dog should be destroyed or be registered on the Index of Exempted Dogs.

In Spain, those wanting to purchase a dangerous breed (Rottweilers, Dobermans, Staffordshire terriers and mastiffs) must first prove that they (the humans, not the dogs) are more than 18 years of age, have no criminal convictions and are mentally and physically capable of controlling the dog. The wannabe owners must go to a special center, where they undergo a physical and psychological assessment by trained professionals. Those deemed worthy are issued a certificate.

Let Your Voice be Heard

In New Jersey, having your dog debarked is illegal and carries a penalty of $15,000 and five years in prison. The law wasn't created to protect dogs; it was enacted to prevent criminals from making their guard dogs quieter so the dogs could sneak up on police and attack them. Whatever the reason, it is a good start—with luck, other states (and countries) will follow New Jersey's example.

 A U.S. poll revealed that 33 percent of dog owners admit they talk to their dog on the phone or leave their pooch messages on the answering machine when they are away.

Break the Chains that Bind

California passed a law in 2006 that prohibits its citizens from chaining up their dogs. Advocates of the anti-tethering law argued that keeping a dog on a leash is inhumane and presents a danger to the public. Keeping a dog chained up makes it more aggressive, they say, because it feels defenseless, knowing it cannot escape if threatened. Statistics show that tethered dogs are more than twice as likely to bite. Anyone violating the anti-tethering law faces a maximum $1000 fine or up to six months in jail.

Bag and Bin It

Throughout the UK, it is against the law not to clean up after your dog when walking in a public place. If you are caught shirking your pooper-scooping responsibilities, you could be fined £40 on the spot and might even face a £500 fine, if the case goes to court and you are found guilty. The only people exempt from the dog fouling law are those who are legally blind and walking with a service dog. Italy has a similar dog-fouling law on the books, but it is virtually unenforceable, thanks to all the stray dogs wandering the streets.

DID YOU KNOW?

Before the law requiring pet owners in New York City to scoop up after their dogs, about 40 million pounds (18 million kilograms) of doggie doodoo were left on the streets each year.

One dog barks at something, the rest bark at him.

–Chinese proverb

STRANGE DOG LAWS

You've gotta wonder if our lawmakers have enough to do. Clearly, the people who thought up some of these dog laws had too much time on their hands.

- In Oklahoma, you'd better restrain yourself from making faces at a dog—you could be fined, arrested or even jailed.

- In Tulsa, Oklahoma, a dog is not allowed to set a paw on private property unless the property owner gives the pooch permission.

- Planning a cultured night out in Chicago? Better leave Fifi at home—in the windy city, taking a French poodle to the opera is illegal.

- In Westport, Massachusetts, dogs are banned from riding in ambulances.

☞ Under no circumstances are cats allowed to chase dogs up telephone poles in International Falls, Minnesota. It's about time someone put those bullying kitties in their place!

☞ You might want to keep Sparky in the house if you live in Danbury, Connecticut; should he get a little frisky with the neighborhood cutie, you are financially responsible and must pay for the abortion, if the pregnant pooch's owners want the procedure done. My question is: Since when do dogs get abortions?

☞ Dogs must not be tied to shade trees in Birmingham, Alabama.

☞ In Ventura County, California, cats and dogs need a permit to have sex. I wonder if that means with each other?

☞ In Illinois, the law dictates that no one can give a lighted cigar to a dog, cat or any other type of pet. Also in Illinois—in Chicago, to be exact—it is illegal to give a dog whisky. Those poor pups don't get to have any fun.

☞ Dogs and cats must make nice in Barber, North Carolina, because it is against the law for them to fight.

☞ In Chicago, a dog that barks for longer than 15 minutes is breaking the law. (Lawmakers in Illinois really must have too much time on their hands.)

☞ In Paulding, Ohio, the law allows a police officer to bite a dog to quiet it. I can't imagine that's a law the police like to put into action.

☞ To meet in groups of three or more on private property in Shawnee, Ohio, dogs need a permit signed by the mayor. Those are your tax dollars at work, folks!

DOG NAMES

In North America, the days of Sparky and Spot are drawing to a close. Pet owners in Canada and the U.S. are now leaning toward human names for their animals, especially their dogs. Psychologists say this trend reflects the important role pets have in our lives—we consider them members of the family.

DID YOU  **KNOW?**

Fido is Latin for "I am faithful."

Top 10 Dog Names in North America

Male—Max, Jake, Buddy, Bear, Bailey, Shadow, Sam, Lucky, Rocky and Buster

Female—Maggie, Bear, Molly, Shadow, Lady, Sadie, Lucky, Lucy, Daisy and Brandy

Popular Names Around the World

France

Male—Andre, Balzac (for French journalist and writer Honoré de Balzac), Camille, Corbie, Damien, Napoleon, Fabien and Romeo

Female—Alette, Angeline, Celeste, Danielle, Dominique, Michelle, Etienne and Juliet

Hawaii

Ailani—high chief
Alana—awakening
Aliikia—queen of the sea
Iolana—to soar like an eagle

Hula—dance
Kale—strong or manly
Kona—golden coast
Keiki—child
Po—night
Wahine—girl

Japan
Chibi—cute and small
Fuji—a type of flower, or Mt. Fuji
Katana—Japanese sword
Kotaro—small child
Honou—flame or fire
Kibou—hope
Riki—strength
Taiyou—sun
Tenshi—angel
Yuuki—courage

Spain
Alonzo—noble
Bonita—pretty
Esteban—crown
Nina—girl
Paz—peace
Pedro—stone or rock
Sancho—honest
Ventura—good fortune
Zori—luck, in Basque

Dog Names by Breed

The name you choose for your dog says as much about you as
it does about the dog's breed and personality. Few people name
their Chihuahuas "Goliath" or their mastiffs "Peewee," for

instance, unless they are being ironic. Following are some of the most popular dog names by breed.

Chihuahua—Baby, Bruiser (no doubt thanks to the film *Legally Blond*), Chica, Honey, Jose, Tiny

Golden Retriever—the two most popular names are Sandy and Goldie; other popular names include Blondie, Buddy, Buster, Ginger and Lucy

Poodle—Bella, Foxy, Gustav, Jacques, Mercedes and Pierre

Rottweiler—Brutus, Draco, Harley, Marley, Rocky, Venus

Sic 'Em, Snookums

Police officers generally choose tough or menacing names for their dogs, to heighten the dog's intimidation factor and ensure that the perpetrator knows the dog means business and is not just some affectionate pooch. I don't know about you, but I'd probably run a lot faster from "Fang" than I would from "Fluffy." Top police dog names include Diesel, Hera, Hercules, Hulk, Rocky and Xena.

DID YOU KNOW?

According to Health Department records in San Francisco, the most common name among dogs that have bitten someone is Rocky.

The dog's kennel is not the place to keep a sausage.

–Malaysian proverb

MUTT MISCELLANEA

Here, for those of you who have always wondered what piloerection is and why dogs have webbed feet, is a collection of mutt minutia that's guaranteed to help you win the next time you have a trivia contest.

A Trial-blazing Pair

A man named Bill Irwin is the only blind hiker to have walked the full length of the Appalachian Trail. He made the record-breaking trek with the help of his guide dog, a German shepherd named Orient.

Get 'Em While They're Hot!

Ever wonder how the hot dog got its name? There are many theories, but one of the most widely known explanations originated in the early 1900s, in New York City. At the Polo Grounds baseball stadium, hot dog vendors would attract attention by shouting "Get your dachshund sausages while they're red hot!" Thomas Aloysius (Tad) Dorgan, a sports cartoonist, apparently drew a cartoon depicting barking dachshund sausages nestled in warm buns, and, because he wasn't sure how to spell dachshund, he named the cartoon "Hot Dog." The cartoon was a huge hit, and thereafter, the meaty snack was rechristened the hot dog.

Twinkle, Twinkle, Bright Dog Star

Sirius, also known as the Dog Star, is the brightest star in our night sky. Sirius is also one of the stars closest to the Earth, which probably goes a long way in explaining why it is one of the brightest. It is bluish white but sometimes has a reddish hue when it is near the horizon. The Dog Star is one of the stars in the constellation Canis Major.

While he was a student at Trinity College in Cambridge, Lord Byron was so annoyed by the school's no-dog policy that he adopted a pet bear in protest.

Hey Baby, What's Your Sign?

The Dog is the 11th sign in the Chinese horoscope. According to this zodiac, those born under the Dog sign are idealistic, loyal, caring, intolerant of injustice and defenders of the little guy. On the down side, they can also be stubborn, narrow-minded, temperamental, moody and distrustful of others. The most compatible match for a Dog is a Tiger or a Horse.

Piloerection is the technical term for what we laypersons usually call "bristling" or "raising of a dog's hackles"; that is, when the hair on a dog's neck stands up, either because of fear or cold. During piloerection, it is the dog's guard hairs that stand up.

Seeing Red

Rage syndrome, often called cocker rage syndrome, is thought to be a nervous illness, but it is not well understood. Dogs afflicted with this syndrome unexpectedly and savagely attack a family member, with no provocation. During the attack, the dog is usually disoriented and unresponsive to everything around it. Rage syndrome differs from simple aggressive or dominant behavior, in that the dog does not display the usual body language used to warn of an attack, and the dog generally is confused afterwards. This syndrome occurs in a few dog breeds but is especially prevalent in solid-colored cocker spaniels (especially males), hence the cocker rage syndrome moniker. It has been suggested that the syndrome is a result of abnormally low levels of serotonin in the dog's brain, which might be the result of a shrinking gene pool in purebred dogs.

What're You Looking At?

Domestic dogs rely less on visual cues than do their wild relatives. Whereas wolves and other canines communicate through various body postures, such as the way the tail is held or the ears are positioned, domestic dogs cannot rely on these physical cues. Many domestic dogs have lost this ability, because they have been selectively bred to have droopy ears, short tails or long coats, all of which make physical cues less distinguishable.

What Long Legs You Have

The tallest dog breeds include the Great Dane, the Irish wolfhound, the Saint Bernard, the English mastiff, the Borzoi, and the Anatolian Karabash. These dogs can grow to be 35 inches (90 centimeters) high at the shoulder.

Mini Mutts

At the other end of the doggie size spectrum are the Chihuahua and the Yorkshire terrier, the smallest dog breeds. Chihuahuas usually grow to about 6 to 10 inches (15 to 25 centimeters) tall and weigh from 2 to 6.5 pounds (1 to 3 kilograms). The Yorky is not much larger, at 6 to 10 inches (20 to 25 centimeters) tall and a whopping 6.5 to 7.5 pounds (3 to 3.5 kilograms).

Built-in Flippers

Some dog breeds have webbed feet! The Newfoundland dog, the field spaniel, the poodle, the Portuguese water dog, the German wirehaired pointer, the otterhound and a variety of retrievers, including the Labrador retriever and the Chesapeake Bay retriever, were originally bred to hunt in or retrieve quarry from the water.

DID YOU KNOW?

An adult dog's head is 20 percent smaller than the head of a wolf of the same weight and body size, a result of the evolutionary changes that dogs underwent when they split from wolves and became domesticated. Some of the changes that make the dog's head smaller are smaller teeth and a different jaw structure.

In Memory of....

Wander the Gettysburg Battlefields and you will find memorials honoring the soldiers who fell during what has come to be known as one of the worst battles in the Civil War. One memorial, the Irish Brigade Monument, includes a sculpture of a life-sized Irish wolfhound. The dog is depicted lying at the base of a Celtic cross, pining for the return of his fallen human companions. An inscription on the monument reads: "This, in the matter of size and structure, truthfully represents the Irish wolfhound, a dog that has been extinct for more than a hundred years." The monument was created in 1888 by William Rudolph O'Donovan.

 Saint Bernards and Newfoundland dogs, two breeds generally considered to be "gentle giants," are classified as dangerous dogs under Italian law.

The Better to Bite You With...

Here are a few interesting dog bite stats for you. In the United States, someone needs medical treatment for a dog bite every 40 seconds, and dog bites cause 18 deaths, on average, every year. More than half of all dog-bite victims are children. Most victims are bitten on the face, but 97 percent of injuries sustained by mail carriers are on the legs.

Statistics show that the dog breeds responsible for most of the documented bites are pit bulls, Rottweilers, German shepherds, huskies, Doberman Pinschers and chow chows. German shepherds are responsible for almost half of all dog bites.

DID YOU KNOW?

A puppy is more likely than an adult dog to inflict damage when it bites.

Out, Out, Damned Dingo

It might not be as impressive as the Great Wall of China, but Australia's dingo fence still deserves a nod of recognition. With a length of more than 3400 miles (5500 kilometers), the fence is one of the longest human constructed barriers in the world, and it is the world's longest fence. Stretching from the town of Jimbour in Queensland to the Great Australian Bight, the fence was originally erected in the early 1880s to keep rabbits out of southern Australia. Sheep ranchers, fed up with losing their animals to dingoes, had the fence modified into a dog-proof barrier in 1914. The wire mesh fence stands more than 6 feet (2 meters) high and extends 13 inches (33 centimeters) underground. It has been relatively successful in keeping dingoes out, but some of the clever pooches have still found their way through.

> *My goal in life is to be as good a person as my dog already thinks I am.*
>
> –Author Unknown

ABOUT THE ILLUSTRATOR

Peter Tyler

Peter is a recent graduate of the Vancouver Film School's Visual Art and Design, and Classical animation programs. Though his ultimate passion is in filmmaking, he is also intent on developing his draftsmanship and storytelling, with the aim of using those skills in future filmic misadventures.

ABOUT THE AUTHOR

Wendy Pirk

Wendy Pirk has been an animal lover for as long as she can remember. As a child, she dreamed of being a veterinarian but changed her mind when she realized how many science classes she would have to take. She decided to become an editor and a writer instead. She solemnly swears that she has never, nor will she ever, dress a dog in a frilly pink tutu, or in any other type of clothing, for that matter.